Walks in MYSTERIOUS OXFORDSHIRE

Laurence Main

Published by Sigma Leisure – an imprint of
Sigma Press, 1 South Oak Lane, Wilmslow, Cheshire SK9 6AR, England.

British Library Cataloguing in Publication Data
A CIP record for this book is available from the British Library.

ISBN: 1-85058-579-2

Typesetting and Design by: Sigma Press, Wilmslow, Cheshire.

Cover photograph: The Rollright Stone Circle (Walk 3)

Maps: Morag Perrott

Photographs: the author

Printed by: MFP Design and Print

Disclaimer: the information in this book is given in good faith and is believed to be correct at the time of publication. No responsibility is accepted by either the author or publisher for errors or omissions, or for any loss or injury howsoever caused. Only you can judge your own fitness, competence and experience.

Preface

This is a book of walks in Oxfordshire, averaging six and a half miles, from and to places of legend, magic, mystery and a sense of belonging to a living land. It has two aims. One is to open the eyes of the walker to the nature of the land he or she sets foot on, so that mutual love can be exchanged as humankind shakes itself awake to the need to live in harmony with Mother Earth. The other is to invite those armchair followers of the New Age fashion and even those most worthy souls who tend their veganic gardens to embrace a little more of the planet, to let their soft feet inform remote areas that they are not neglected and to allow places where the spirit has survived more strongly to work through us.

Being brought up in Oxford, the river goddess Isis springs to mind. She is here, of course, as is Old Father Thames below the sacred grove on Castle Hill at Wittenham Clumps. But I prefer to dedicate this book to Rhiannon, who watched over me as I walked and who rode in the nursery-rhyme to Banbury Cross. At the other end of the county, her white horse is carved on the hillside above Uffington. I hadn't realised how much of Oxfordshire is the realm of the Great Queen and the daughter of the Lord of Annwn.

Oddly enough, Rhiannon appeared to me in a dream many miles virtually due west, on the sacred peak of Carn Ingli in Pembrokeshire. She cupped her hands to form a chalice with a corresponding celestial cup above. Her fingers stuck out of the ground in a circle and these became the standing stones of a stone circle, which I saw from above, as if flying.

This was, of course, only a dream – but who knows what you might experience in Mysterious Oxfordshire?

Laurence Main

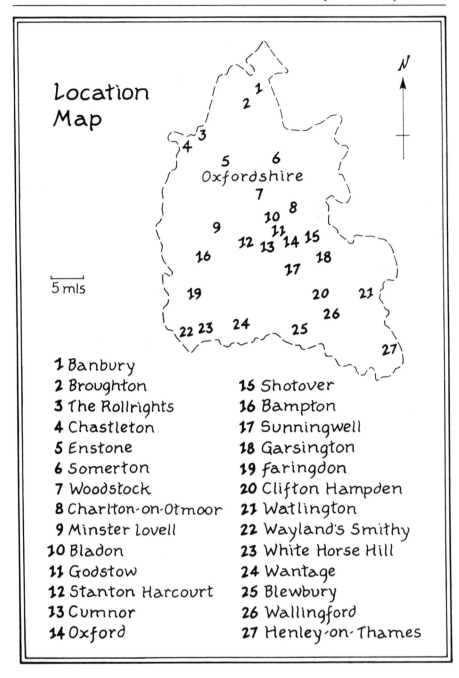

Location Map

Oxfordshire

5 mls

1 Banbury
2 Broughton
3 The Rollrights
4 Chastleton
5 Enstone
6 Somerton
7 Woodstock
8 Charlton-on-Otmoor
9 Minster Lovell
10 Bladon
11 Godstow
12 Stanton Harcourt
13 Cumnor
14 Oxford
15 Shotover
16 Bampton
17 Sunningwell
18 Garsington
19 Faringdon
20 Clifton Hampden
21 Watlington
22 Wayland's Smithy
23 White Horse Hill
24 Wantage
25 Blewbury
26 Wallingford
27 Henley-on-Thames

Contents

Introduction

Walking in Oxfordshire

Oxfordshire makes an attractive destination for ramblers taking a day out from London. Not that Oxford feels any inferiority to London. It's close enough for convenient commuting but far enough away to resist inclusion in the South-East.

There are many aspects to the county – contrasting landscapes meet here to offer a hotchpotch of scenery. There may be no mountains, but there are excellent footpaths which won't overtire the walker. None of the walks in this book is really strenuous – there are no mountains in Oxfordshire – and all walks in this book should be within the capabilities of anyone of average fitness. Allow about one hour for every two miles, which should enable short breaks to be made.

Always equip yourself with good walking boots (I wear non-leather boots when not going in bare feet), an anorak, some food and drink in a rucksack and a torch with batteries may prove useful – but don't start so late that you end up walking in the dark. Do take the required Ordnance Survey Pathfinder or Explorer (1:25,000 scale) maps and a good compass and know how to use them.

Oxfordshire: history and legend

Oxford was twice the capital of England (during the Civil War and the Plague) and Hitler wanted to make it his capital in the event that Germany conquered Britain. Perhaps he knew that the druids reckoned this was the navel of Britain. Whatever the basis for this claim, Banbury, with its famous cakes and major food industry, could justly claim to represent the stomach.

Wessex has historical claims to the south of the county, with the sacred stones at the entrance to Wayland's Smithy reminiscent of Avebury and Stonehenge. The limestone and ironstone hills of the Cotswolds in the west and north-west are surmounted by their own ridgeway, leading to the classic stone circle of Rollright.

Turn to the Chiltern Hills in the east of the county and you are patrolling an ancient border, where King Arthur's knights watered their black horses at the sites of public houses now commemorated in their names. We are on the fringe of history here and many of Oxford's mysteries do belong to the era of written records. Fair Rosamund really was Henry II's mistress; Amy Robsart's death did cause an Elizabethan scandal; Roger Bacon was an alchemist and astronomer who lived under the threat of a charge of heresy from the Roman Catholic Church; if there really was a skeleton in a secret room at Minster Lovell, we can guess it belonged to 'Lovell the dogge'; Mary Blandy's corpse lies next to the father she either wittingly or unwittingly poisoned at Henley-on-Thames.

Oxford itself has a host of ghosts which can be identified. The most poignant story is of the Tear Drop room in Wallingford. Other monuments and legends loom out of the mists of antiquity to perplex the modern mind. What do we make of the lost giant of Shotover? Was he related to Wayland the Smith? Did Sumerians or Trojans cut the turf maze at Somerton? Is it the Turning Castle of Arianrhod? Was Fair Roz the King's prize at the centre of a similar labyrinth at Woodstock? Do the Morrismen dance to help restore fertility to Mother Earth? Is the garlanded cross in the church at Charlton-on-Otmoor a symbol of the goddess? Were two lovers in a hay-field a fertility sacrifice on the Eve of Lughnasadh at Stanton Harcourt? Why should a church display a Shiel-na-gig, as in Oxford's St Michael's in the Northgate? All of these are encountered in the walks in this book

Ley lines and dowsing

Go to Oxford's Carfax, or follow the route in this book to Chastleton (Walk 4) and it's easy to recognise, if not understand, a ley.

One special alignment linked with great warriors involves the Column of Victory (Walk 7) and Sir Winston Churchill's grave (Walk 10). Jarn Mound (Walk 17), Faringdon Folly (Walk 19) and the Memorial Cross to Lord Wantage (Walk 24) suggest that either lost knowledge has survived to the 20th century or we are still being guided unconsciously to erect monuments at appropriate sacred spots. Check out Hamish Miller's and Paul Broadhurst's findings in their book "The Sun and the Serpent" at Clifton Hampden, Churn Knob and Garsington. Dowse the line of the spirit path from the King Stone at Rollright to Banbury Cross. Much primary research remains to be done on leys but a small band of dedicated people keep adding to our knowledge. Paul Devereux in particular has raised the profile of leys and other Earth Mysteries with orthodox academics and, although a friend, he won't thank me for carrying my dowsing rods on these expeditions. Actually, I've found young archaelogists quite happy to trust them. They give the wrong image to the modern *Ley Hunter* magazine, however, so please don't tell Danny Sullivan, its new editor, that I used them. I'm not clever enough to explain why, but I do find that they work for me. Perhaps I spend too much time walking along leys and dreaming at sacred sites and not enough talking in pubs and reading books. You can get details of the Ley Hunter magazine by writing to PO Box 258, Cheltenham, GL53 OHR, or telephone 01242 261680.

Public Transport

None of these walks are impossible to reach without a car. I used public transport to reach all of them with one exception, where I am grateful for Penny Allen's driving and company. That one (White Horse Hill) has often been reached by bus by me in the past, however. You may have to walk a few extra miles to reach Blewbury from Didcot railway station and do the Chastleton walk when you are half way around the Rollrights circuit, but this is a small price to pay for not taking another car into the countryside. The motor-car is one of the chief enemies of the living earth and it makes nonsense of your reverence for nature if you add to the pollution and demand for more roads. The bus or train company, and the local community, will be glad of your support.

The Ramblers

Each walk in this book follows rights of way to which you, as a member of the public, has unrestricted access. These are public footpaths, bridleways and by-ways as well as lanes and roads. When surveyed, all these routes were free of obstructions. Such a statement is a tribute to the work of the Oxfordshire Area of the Ramblers' Association and to the County Council's Rights of Way officers. Should you discover any problems on rights of way in Oxfordshire, send full details (including grid references) to the Ramblers' Association at 1/5 Wandsworth Road, London, SW8 2XX, and to the Right of Way Officer, Oxfordshire County Council, Department of Leisure and Arts, Central Library, Westgate, Oxford, OX1 1DJ (tel. 01865 810808). Do remember that the physical landscape is changing all the time, for example, as hedgerows are grubbed up and fields amalgamated. Keep to the path and always regard it as a privilege to walk across someone else's land; in that way we can build an atmosphere of co-operation, rather than confrontation, in the countryside.

The Country Code

¤   Guard against all risk of fire.

¤   Leave gates as you find them.

¤   Keep dogs under proper control.

¤   Avoid damaging fences, hedges and walls.

¤   Keep to paths across farmland.

¤   Leave no litter.

¤   Safeguard water supplies.

¤   Protect wildlife, wild plants and trees.

¤   Go carefully on country roads.

¤   Respect the life of the countryside.

1. Banbury

Route: Banbury – Oxford Canal – Bodicote – Salt Way – The Bretch – Banbury.

Distance: 8.5 miles. Moderate.

Maps: OS Pathfinders 1022 Banbury (North) and 1045 Brackley & Banbury (South), OS Landranger 151 Stratford-upon-Avon.

Start: Banbury railway station (SP 462404)

Access: Trains run to Banbury from Oxford, London (both Paddington and Marylebone) and Birmingham, with many through services from farther afield. There are also many local bus services (tel. 01865 810405 for details).

A Fine Lady on a White Horse

'Ride-a-cock-horse to Banbury Cross.
To see a fine lady on a white horse.
With rings on her fingers and bells on her toes.
She shall have music wherever she goes.'

This most famous of nursery rhymes commemorates the Celtic goddess Rhiannon. She appears in the First Branch of the Mabinogi riding on a white horse and is equated with the European horse-goddess Epona. The Celtic name Rhiannon may refer to Rigantona (Great Queen) or to the maiden (rhiain) of the Underworld (Annwn). Her character is that of a generous and long-suffering mother-goddess who is the mother of a hero. The magical singing birds of Rhiannon enable men to forget their sorrows. She is also linked to the fertility of the land and it is known that a fair was held on Good Fridays at the Giant's Cave, while sunrise at Beltane (May Day) was greeted with festivities on Crouch Hill. The modern cross is situated where Banbury's famous horse fair was held.

Banbury Cross

Puritans destroyed the original crosses, of which Banbury had three. Their whereabouts are known approximately and the cross that was erected in 1859 to mark the occasion of Queen Victoria's wedding the previous year would appear to be on a straight line between two of them, the Bread Cross in Butchers Row and a White Cross in West Bar. The third cross (Market Cross) was in Cornhill, not far from the Bread Cross. The White Cross probably had the oldest pedigree, being perhaps on the site of an ancient white stone.

The line linking the Bread Cross, the 1859 cross and the White Cross kept cropping up as I dowsed for leys or spirit paths in the course of walking the routes in this book. It extends to St Mary's Church, Broughton (Walk 2), clips the north-western corner of Broughton Castle's moat and continues to the King Stone at Rollright (Walk 3).

Another major alignment runs east-west, connecting it with the equinoxes. In this respect it is interesting to note that the sun is a central feature in Banbury's coat of arms and the town's motto is 'Dominus nobis sol et scutum' (The Lord is our sun and shield). The name Banbury is most probably derived from Bambury, meaning 'sacred to the sun'. There is a Bambury (sometimes spelt Banbury) Stone on Bredon Hill in south Worcestershire, along the east-west line from Banbury. Brian Hoggard investigated this alignment in *The Ley Hunter* no 125 and took it from British Camp on the Malvern Hills in the west to Bambury Stone and Elmley Castle on Bredon Hill, through a significant crossroads at Hinton-on-the-Green and the cross at the edge of Saintbury before visiting Dover's Hill, where the Cotswolds Olympics were held. The line then takes in Castle Hill at the northern edge of Brailes Hill and there is an old tale that Bredon Hill and Brailes Hill were connected by a burial path. If Banbury was a crossroads for spirit paths, it also marked the junction of primitive trackways, notably the Jurassic Way (leading to the Rollright stones) and the Salt Way, used to carry salt from Droitwich to London. Giant's Cave is a pit near the junction of these two routes and a tunnel legend links it with Broughton Castle.

The Walk

1. Take the station access road across the bridge over the River Cherwell, reach a junction and go ahead across the road by a pelican crossing. Enter a small park to follow a metalled path to the towpath of the Oxford Canal on your left. Turn left to walk with the canal on your right and walk south of Banbury. Ignoring swing bridges, reach a fixed bridge and turn right to cross the canal by it and follow a track up to the A423 road.

2. Cross the A423 and take Broad Gap ahead. Reach a T-junction and turn right along High Street, becoming White Post Road. Pass playing fields on your left and turn left along the Salt Way, here waymarked as the Banbury Fringe Circular Walk. Continue across the A361 and eventually emerge from the Salt Way at the B4035 road.

3. Cross the B4035 and take waymarked steps down into scrubland, where a diversion to the left would bring you to the big pit known as Giant's Cave. Go right with the waymarked Banbury Fringe Circular Walk, starting parallel to the road on your right before bearing left at a track with the waymarked route taking steps up to a field. Go left and turn right in the corner to follow a path at first between fields, then along the left-hand edge of a field.

4. Go ahead over a waymarked stile in the top left corner of the field. Pass through a belt of trees to emerge in the top corner of the next field and bear right downhill. Turn right in the bottom corner and follow the waymarked path through patchy woodland.

5. Reach a waymarked path junction in the corner of a field and let the Banbury Fringe Circular Walk go left as you take the path ahead, running beside a hedge on your left. Bear left through a gap in the hedge in the corner and continue with a hedge on your right.

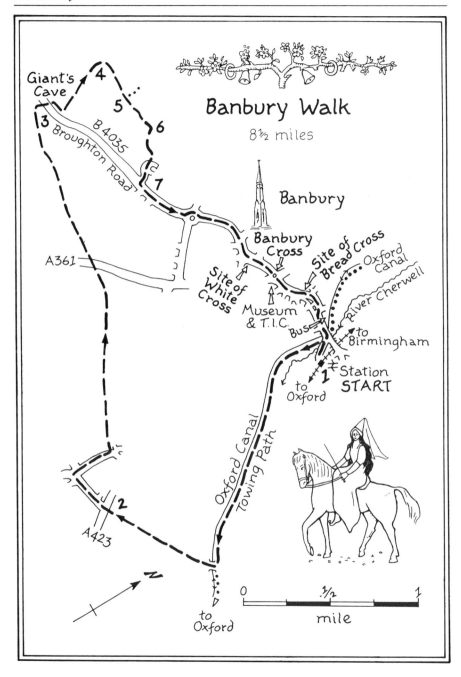

Giant's Cave

4

5

6

3
B 4035
Broughton Road

7

A361

A423

2

N

Banbury Walk

8½ miles

Banbury

Banbury Cross

Site of White Cross

Site of Bread Cross

Oxford Canal

River Cherwell

Museum & T.I.C.

Bus

to Birmingham

Station
START

1

to Oxford

Oxford Canal Towing Path

to Oxford

0   ½   1

mile

6. Turn right in the corner of the field, go ahead with a hedge on your right and turn left at a corner. Continue beside a hedge on your right in the next field and approach a television mast, ahead on your left. Turn right to the top of Balmoral Avenue and go downhill.

7. Go left along Broughton Road back into Banbury, going ahead at a roundabout. Fork left up West Bar Street, passing the site of the old White Cross, to reach the Victorian cross. The highly-recommended museum and Tourist Information Centre are ahead on your right. Go ahead along High Street and turn left opposite Ottakar's Bookshop to the Butchers Row and the site of the Bread Cross. Continue past the bus station and across the bridge over the canal to return to the railway station, on your right.

2. Broughton

Route: Broughton – Broughton Castle – North Newington – Broughton.

Distance: 3 miles. Moderate.

Maps: OS Pathfinder 1045 Brackley & Banbury (South), OS Landranger 151 Stratford-upon-Avon

Start: Saye & Sele Arms, Broughton (SP 421384)

Access: Buses run to Broughton from Banbury on weekdays. Telephone 01295 768292 or 01865 810405 for details.

A Tunnel Legend

St Mary's Church, Broughton, is where I first became aware of the ley or spirit path linking the King Stone, Rollright, with the cross at Banbury. Sheltering from the rain there, I met a farmer from a neighbouring county whose wife was a seventh daughter of a seventh daughter and had led him to investigate earth mysteries. We both dowsed the same ley before opening the maps to plot its course from our compass bearing. It went through the site of the old White Cross, the Victorian cross and the old Bread Cross in Banbury. In

St Mary's Church

the other direction the line led straight to the King Stone, Roll-right. We were both strangers to the area and hadn't thought of this connection. I had in mind the tunnel legend linking the Giant's Cave on the edge of Banbury with the castle at Broughton, but the ley missed this. Try dowsing around St Mary's Church for yourself, then dowse at other spots along this ley, such as Banbury Cross (Walk 1) and the King Stone, Rollright (Walk 3), where my dowsing rod confirmed the same alignment. Broughton Castle was and still is the home of the Fiennes Family and Puritans met there during the Civil War. Telephone 01295 262624 for details of opening times.

The Walk

1. Face the Saye & Sele Arms and go left. Turn right along the path to St Mary's Church and continue through the gate at the west end of the churchyard. Take the drive ahead but when this bends right, go ahead uphill through parkland, bearing very slightly right, for 250 yards, then turn left to aim for the top end of a patch of woodland.

2. Take a stile 20 yards to the right of the corner formed by the wood and a fence. Follow the fieldpath to a barn, ignore a stile to the left of this and take a gate ahead. Turn right to walk with a track up the right-hand edge of a field, cross a lane, bear left to a stile, cross it and continue up the right-hand edge of the next field.

3. Take the gate in the corner and walk beside a hedge on your right. Turn right through a gate in the hedge to descend diagonally to the bottom left corner of this field. Turn left and go along the right-hand edge of the next field.

4. Turn right along the pavement of what becomes the Main Street of North Newington. Pass the Blinking Owl pub on your right and bear right with the Banbury Road. Immediately after passing the

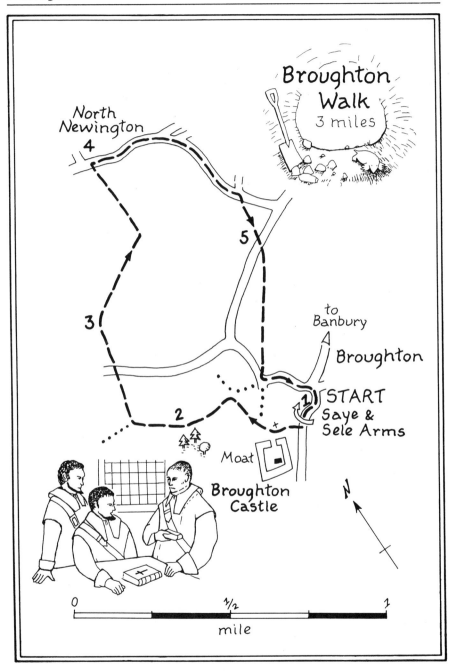

Broughton Walk
3 miles

North Newington
4

5

to Banbury

Broughton

START
Saye & Sele Arms

3

2

Moat

Broughton Castle

N

0   ½   1
mile

access lane to Broughton Farm on your left, bear right over a stile
and follow a path between fields.

5. Bear right across a lane and over a stile. Cut across the corner
    of a field to a stile on your right, cross it and a subsequent lane
    and footbridge to maintain your direction through a field to reach
    a gate in the far corner. This gives access to a road, which you go
    left along to return to Broughton.

3. The Rollrights

Route: Bus Stop at turning for Rollright on A34 – Little Rollright – Salford – Rollright stone circle – Bus Stop at turning for Rollright on A34.

Distance: 5 miles. Strenuous.

Maps: OS Pathfinders 1044 Moreton-in-Marsh & Hook Norton and 1068 Chipping Norton & Adlestrop, OS Landrangers 151 Stratford-upon-Avon, 163 Cheltenham & Cirencester and 164 Oxford.

Start: Bus Stop at turning for Rollright on the A34.

Access: Bus no X50 runs daily between Oxford and Stratford-upon-Avon (tel. 01788 535555 for details), while there is a bus (no 3) on Wednesdays only from Chipping Norton (tel. 01608 662934 for details) and a bus (no 1) on Tuesdays only between Banbury and Moreton-in-Marsh (tel. 01608 50876 for details). Telephone 01865 810405 for further information on buses. Please note that this is a request stop.

A Petrified King and his Army

A legendary king marched here at the head of his army. Five of his knights stood apart, whispering treachery, while the king led his loyal men up the ridge, where a witch confronted him:

> 'Seven long strides thou shalt take
> And if Long Compton thou can see
> King of England thou shalt be'.

As the king strode forward anticipating the view over Long Compton, a mound rose up to obscure it and the witch shrieked:

> 'As Long Compton thou canst not see
> King of England thou shalt not be.
> Rise up, stick, and stand still, stone,
> For King of England thou shalt be none.
> Thou and thy men hoar stones shall be
> And I myself an eldern tree.'

The king was turned into the King Stone, actually just inside

The Rollright Stone Circle

Warwickshire (the road is the county boundary). The fairies dance around this on certain nights. His loyal men were turned into the circle of 77 (or is it 76?) stones. At least one dowser reckons this circle marks where fragments of a meteorite are embedded in the earth. The treacherous knights form the stones known as the Whispering Knights (and sounds have been heard coming from them at full moon).

The Rollright stones were the subject of some exasperating ultrasonic monitoring by the Dragon Project in 1980. Paul Devereux, then editor of *The Ley Hunter*, did take a startling infra-red photograph showing a glow at the top of the King Stone one dawn in 1979.

Alfred Watkins linked the old legend to a ley he outlined in his *The Old Straight Track*, running from Long Compton Church through Rollright stone circle to Chipping Norton castle and church. A ley described by Paul Devereux and Ian Thomson in *The Ley Hunter's Companion* runs to Madmarston Hill camp (SP 386389) and is tantalisingly close to the direction of the summer solstice sunrise. My own dowsing confirmed a ley running south to Uffington white horse (Walk 23), taking in Faringdon's Folly (Walk 19). Oxfordshire ley hunter Roy Cooper first alerted me to this ley and extends it northwards to Brailes Hill (see Walk 1 about the Banbury – Bambury Stone ley).

Other leys I dowsed linked the King Stone, the stone circle and the Whispering Knights with each other, the King Stone with Banbury Cross (see Walks 1 and 2), the Whispering Knights with Hook Norton Church and the stone circle with the churches at Todenham and Stretton-on-Fosse.

The Walk

1. Alight from the bus at the staggered crossroads where, as you face north going away from Oxford, the road for Little Rollright is on your left and the road for Great Rollright is on your right. Turn south to walk back towards Oxford along the verge of the A34. Look for a narrow gully on your right up which you will take a footpath. If you overshoot this, you'll come to steps for the footpath on the other, left-hand or eastern, side of the road. Emerge from the gully in the corner of a field. Go ahead, as waymarked, along its left-hand edge, then along the right-hand edge of the following field. Cross a track to maintain your direction through another field and the next, where the Whispering Knights can be seen away to your right. Continue along the left-hand edge of the next field and descend to a road.

2. Cross the road and take the waymarked path ahead to pass Little Rollright church away to your right. Cross a lane, go left and soon turn right to pass barns and go ahead, as waymarked, uphill to a stile just to the left of a kink in the field boundary ahead. Go ahead with a hedge on your right.

3. Take the stile or kissing gate in the corner to follow the path

through a plantation of trees. Go ahead, as waymarked, across a track and along the right-hand edge of a field. Turn right through a waymarked gate and immediately turn left to walk with the hedge on your left to a waymarked gate giving admission to another plantation of trees. Emerge from this by crossing a stile and bearing left through a field to a stile in the hedge opposite. Continue over another stile beside a gate and through a field to a stile leading to a lane.

4. Go right and almost immediately leave the lane by turning right up a track which begins by following the right-hand edge of a field. Climb with the hedged track which becomes a metalled lane shortly before joining a road.

5. Go right along the road and soon pass a turning to Little Compton on your left. Go ahead at a crossroads and reach the Rollright stone circle on your right, soon followed by the King Stone on your left. Reach the A34, where the bus for Oxford should be halted by making a clear signal requesting it to on the other side of the road.

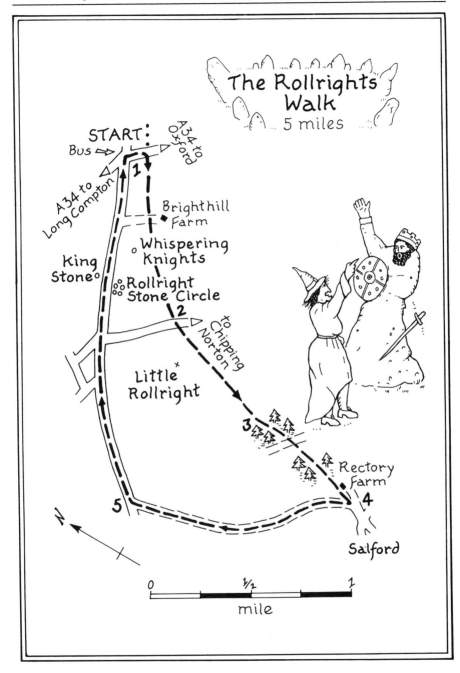

The Rollrights Walk
5 miles

```
┌─────────────────────────────────────────────────────┐
│                                                       │
│                4. Chastleton            ˙             │
│                                                       │
└─────────────────────────────────────────────────────┘
```

Route: Cross Hands Inn – St Peter's Church, Cornwell – Chastleton
Barrow Fort – Chastleton House – Cross Hands Inn.

Distance: 5 miles. Moderate.

Maps: OS Pathfinder 1068 Chipping Norton & Adlestrop, OS Landranger
163 Cheltenham & Cirencester.

Start: Cross Hands Inn, Salford Hill (SP 270289).

Access: Yes, this is a challenge by public transport. I did this walk on
the same day as the Rollrights (Walk 3), using about one mile of road to
link Walk 3's direction point 5 with the Cross Hands Inn (go left, instead
of right for the Rollrights). Taking this route in isolation, there are buses
on Tuesdays only, no 1 running between Banbury and Moreton-in-Marsh
(tel. 01608 50876 for details), with no 6 going between Charlbury and
Moreton-in-Marsh and no 7 between Woodstock and Moreton-in-Marsh
(tel. 01608 677415 for details). Telephone 01865 810405 for further
information on buses. Please note that this is a request stop.

A Spirit Path

Walk (and dowse) a section of a ley or spirit path from St Peter's
Church, Cornwell to St Mary's Church, Chastleton. This line can
be extended to Chastleton House, where a spirited lady saved her
husband from capture during the Civil War. Arthur Jones, grand-
son of the Witney woollen merchant, Walter Jones, who bought
the estate off Robert Catesby, of Gunpowder Plot fame, in 1602
and built the fine Jacobean house, fought for King Charles II at
the Battle of Worcester in 1651. Fleeing here after the defeat, he
was followed by Cromwell's men. He hid in a secret room while
his wife gave his pursuers drinks laced with laudanum, which
put them asleep. Choosing the best of the Roundheads' horses,
her husband then rode to another secret place.

Chastleton Barrow Fort is an Iron Age hillfort and the ley,

Chastleton House

characteristically, glances the edge of its ancient earthwork. The road from Cornwell Manor to the junction with the A436, where you go ahead for the hillfort, coincides with the ley or spirit path.

The Walk

1. Face the Cross Hands Inn from the other side of the A44 and go right (towards Oxford). Turn right down a lane signposted as part of the Oxfordshire Cycleway.

2. Turn right to take a signposted footpath through a kissing gate beside a fieldgate. Descend to cross a stream then bear left uphill to St Peter's Church, Cornwell. Take its enclosed access path from the western end and turn right to cross a stile beside a signpost. Turn left immediately to pass Cornwell House on your left, then bear left over another stile beside a signpost to go through an orchard and reach a road.

3. Go right along the road and go straight ahead at a T-junction with the A436. Follow a path along the right-hand edge of a field, go ahead through a gate to cross the fort and leave by a gate opposite. Walk with a fence on your left and continue through a series of gates. Cross an access lane and take a small metal gate ahead to walk parallel to a road on your left. Eventually come to a gate between a wall and a fence ahead to reach another lane at a cattle grid.

4. Turn left to a junction and go right to follow the road to Chastleton House. Return to the junction.

5. Turn left to cross the cattle grid again and follow the lane to the A44. Go right along its verge to return to the Cross Hands Inn.

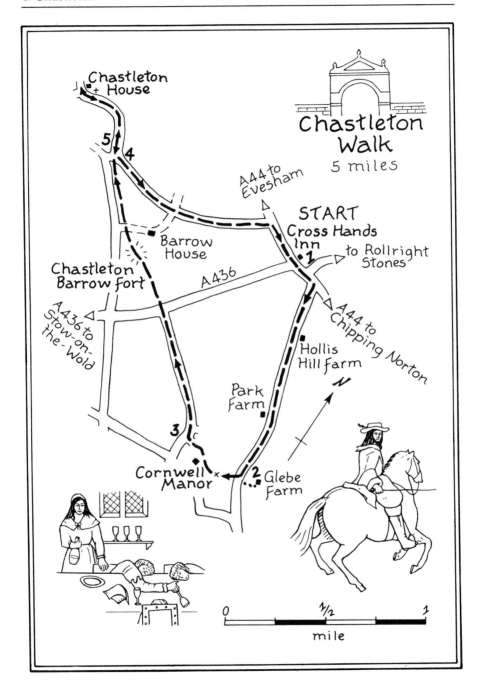

Chastleton
House

5

4

A44 to
Evesham

Chastleton
Walk
5 miles

START
Cross Hands
Inn
1

to Rollright
Stones

Barrow
House

Chastleton
Barrow Fort

A436

A436 to
Stow-on-
the-Wold

A44 to
Chipping Norton

Hollis
Hill Farm

N

Park
Farm

3

Cornwell
Manor

2 Glebe
Farm

0   ½   1
mile

---

5. Enstone

Route: Enstone – Church Enstone – Heythrop Park – Hoar Stone – Enstone.

Distance: 6 miles. Moderate.

Maps: OS Pathfinder 1068 Chipping Norton & Adlestrop, OS Landranger 164 Oxford.

Start: Bus Shelter, The Green, Enstone (SP 377242).

Access: Buses run to Enstone daily, from Oxford and Chipping Norton. Telephone 01608 677322 for details of no 70; Telephone 01865 727000 for details of nos 20, 20A, 20B & 20C, Bus no X50 also comes from Stratford-upon-Avon (tel.01788 535555 for details). There is also the National Express coach no 511 from Great Malvern (tel. 0990 808080 for details). Telephone 01865 810405 for more information on buses.

The Hoar Stone

The Hoar Stone is actually a pile of stones which formed a neolithic burial chamber. Spirit paths or leys seem to converge or radiate from it, just as the junction of five roads made the Church Enstone and Neat Enstone complex an important coaching centre, with six inns. Sacred pathways obviously meet here. I dowsed the most important ley as bearing 84 degrees (88 less 4 for magnetic variation). This links with Knollbury in the west, but if the bearing had been 88 degrees it would have led east to another hoar stone at SP 458241. Other leys dowsed took bearings of 353 (357-4), running south to the hillfort in Eynsham Hall Park (SP 394115), and 174 (178 less 4 for magnetic variation).

The Walk

1. Go behind the bus shelter to the back of the Green, with the telephone box on your left. Go ahead along a lane until it bends left. Take the signposted path ahead to Church Enstone, going through a kissing gate beside a fieldgate and descending to cross a footbridge, a board-walk and another footbridge.

2. Climb steps and go ahead through a field. Take a stile in the corner and follow the fence around on your left to a stile giving access to an enclosed path leading to a road. Cross this and go ahead, bearing right to St Kenelm's Church. Pass this church on your right as you take the signposted path for Heythrop. Ignore a path on your right at a junction. Go ahead through a small wooden gate, then a tall metal gate and over a stile. Cross a track to emerge over a stile into a field.

3. Go around the left-hand edge of the field, turning right in the first corner. Go ahead over a stile in the bottom left corner of the field and maintain this direction through the next field to a stile beside a gate where the hedge opposite turns. Continue through the next field, going towards its far left corner.

The boardwalk between Enstone and Church Enstone

4. Take the stile beside a gate 50 yards to the right of the corner. Pass a gate in the fence on your left. Go ahead over stepping-stones and bear right over a stile, as signposted. Go right along a waymarked grass track past woodland, soon forking right at a signpost.

5. Keep right with the woodland track and fork right at the next signpost to go down to a stream and walk upstream with it on your right. Pass an artificial waterfall and a lily pond. Ignore a bridge and continue past a lake on your right.

6. Turn right over an impressive stone bridge along a drive signposted as a footpath. Continue to a road and turn right.

7. Turn right at a T-junction, as signposted for Enstone. Reach the B4030, turn right along its pavement for 30 yards, then take a lane on your left, marked unsuitable for heavy goods vehicles.

8. Turn right over a stile beside a gate and go ahead with the signposted footpath. Rejoin your outward route and retrace your steps to the bus shelter on Enstone Green. Go left and fork right to take the road up to a crossroads where the Hoar Stone is ahead on your right.

9. Retrace your steps back down to Enstone.

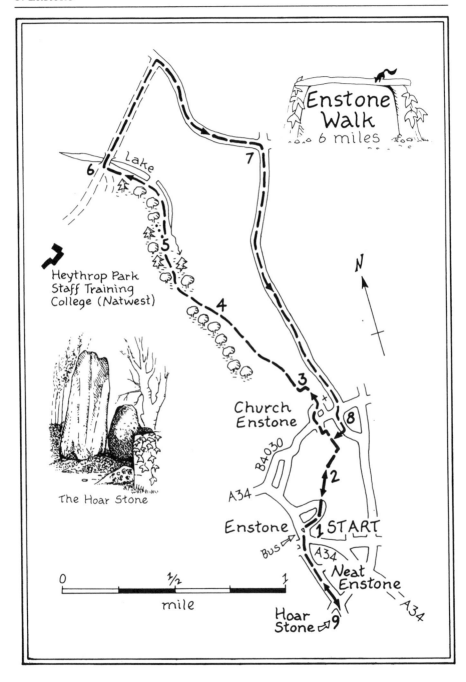

Enstone
Walk
~ 6 miles

7

6 Lake

5

Heythrop Park
Staff Training
College (Natwest)

4

N

3

Church
Enstone

8

The Hoar Stone

B4030

A34

2

Enstone

1 START

Bus

A34

Neat
Enstone

A34

0   ½   1

mile

Hoar
Stone 9

6. Somerton

Route: Heyford station – Oxford Canal – Somerton – Maze – Upper Heyford – Lower Heyford – Heyford station.

Distance: 10 miles. Easy.

Maps: OS Pathfinder 1069 Bicester, OS Landranger 164 Oxford.

Start: Heyford railway station (SP 483247).

Access: Trains run to Heyford from Oxford and Banbury.

Troy Town

Mazes are linked with Troy, perhaps because the Trojans built their town in concentric rings. After the fall of Troy, around 1100 BC, Brutus led some survivors to found a New Troy in Britain and, according to Mary Caine in 'The Glastonbury Zodiac – Key to the Mysteries of Britain', this maze is special. The name Somerton is derived from Sumer-town and refers to the Summerians, Cimmerians or Cymry who came from the east under Hu Gadarn, the solar hero, Their chief base was Somerset, whose ancient capital was Somerton. Hu Gadarn was the original John Bull, suggesting a link with the Age of Taurus, which probably ended in 2330 BC. Hu (pronounced 'He') is said to have come from Defrobane, in the region of the modern Istanbul, near Troy. Troy was known as the Ilium or pelvis, meaning cradle of civilization. The sacked Troy rose again elsewhere out of the ashes like a phoenix, with the Phoenicians, who traded with Britain. This is a myth in the real sense, being an eternal truth. Truth and trust are two words linked with Troy. It may be that Brutus's wisemen or magi founded the first Oxfordshire university here, before it moved down the Cherwell.

Oxfordshire had other mazes, of course, notably on Tadmarton Heath, between the Rollrights and Banbury, at Temple Cowley and the one made famous by Fair Roz at Woodstock. This is the survivor, however.

The Oxford Canal, North of Lower Heyford

It is 60ft 6ins by 51ft 6ins (18.3m by 15.6m) and cut in the turf opposite Troy Farm, whose name goes back to at least the 16th century. Jeff and Deb Saward have documented lost mazes in their magazine *Caerdroia*, while Nigel Pennick's book *Mazes and Labyrinths* is an authoritative tome. Virgins were known to stand in the centre of mazes waiting for their young men to reach them (after overcoming obstacles?) and carry them out. The labyrinth also represented the maze of life and the overcoming of animal passions through increasing consciousness. The twists and turns of the maze are like the spirals of the Turning Castle or Caer Sidi of Arianrhod, the Queen of Heaven, whose palace was the Milky Way. Arianrhod's Zodiacal Silver Wheel suggests that the maze reflects the revolving stars. The Greek equivalent of Arianrhod was Ariadne, who helped Theseus to escape from the labyrinth. To the Celts, Theseus was Esus, the Divine Essence, God in Man (hence the easy acceptance of Jesus by the Druids). Theseus, of course, had to kill the Minotaur, half-bull, half-man (his animal passions).

The Walk

1. Gain access to the towpath of the Oxford Canal from Heyford railway station and go left to walk with the canal on your right. Follow the towpath under a railway bridge.

2. Turn right to take a road bridge over the canal and enter Somerton. Fork left in the centre of the village and look out for Troy Farm on your left in about one and a half miles. Just before coming level with its buildings, notice the turf maze or troy town on your right.

3. Turn right along a signposted public footpath, approach the perimeter fence of the airfield recently vacated by the USAF and turn right to walk parallel to it on your left. Reach farm buildings and turn left with a track to find the airfield's perimeter fence once more on your left. Turn right with this fence but when it turns left, go straight ahead down to a road.

4. Go left to Upper Heyford. Pass Mill Lane and the Barley Mow pub on your right. Turn right along High Street, passing the Three Horseshoes pub on your left. Fork left along School Lane and pass the green on your right.

5. Before reaching the church, turn left along a signposted path to cross a field to a kissing-gate giving access to a track. Go left along this to a junction and turn right with a concrete track. Cross a stile to the left of a gate across this, walk with a hedge on your left, go ahead over another stile to the right of a gate across the track and continue towards another gate. Bear left before it to go over a stile and along the right-hand edge of a field. Turn right to the foot of the field and go left past reed beds on your right.

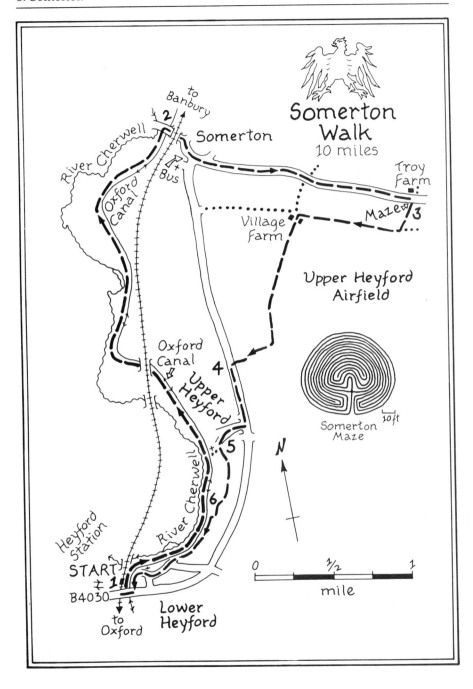

Somerton
Walk
10 miles

to Banbury

Somerton

River Cherwell

Oxford Canal

Bus

Troy Farm

Village Farm

Maze

Upper Heyford Airfield

Oxford Canal

Upper Heyford

Somerton Maze

10 ft

N

Heyford Station

River Cherwell

START

B4030

to Oxford

Lower Heyford

0   ½   1

mile

6. Walk with the canal on your right and cross a stile to enter a playing field. Continue to a lane and go left into Lower Heyford. Turn right along Freehold Street and right in Market Square to pass the Bell Inn on your right. Bear left along Church Lane to pass St Mary's Church on your right. Go ahead along an enclosed path, emerge to walk with the canal on your right and follow a waymarked path which bears left to a road. Go right to cross a bridge over the canal and reach the railway station.

7. Woodstock

Route: Old Woodstock – Column of Victory – Fair Rosamund's Well – Akeman Street – Old Woodstock.

Distance: 6 miles. Easy.

Maps: OS Pathfinder 1092 Woodstock, OS Landranger 164 Oxford.

Start: Rose and Crown, Old Woodstock (SP 441172).

Access: Buses nos 20, 20A, 20B and 20C link Woodstock with Oxford and Chipping Norton (tel. 01865 727000 for details). Bus no X50 goes through Woodstock on its way between Oxford and Stratford-uponAvon (tel. 01788 535555 for details), while bus no 70 links Woodstock with Oxford and Enstone (tel. 01608 677322 for details). Telephone 01865 810405 for details of all bus services in Oxfordshire.

Fair Rosamund's Well and the Column of Victory

This walk takes you past two sites which are the subjects of other walks. Read more about Rosamund Clifford in Walk 11 (Godstow) and about the Warrior Path linking the Column of Victory with Sir Winston Churchill's birthplace and grave in Walk 10 (Bladon). The Column of Victory in Blenheim Park was finished in 1730 at a cost of £3,000. It is 134 feet high and has a lead statue of John Churchill, first Duke of Marlborough, at the top. The site of Woodstock's old royal manor house, together with nearly 1800 acres of parkland, was conferred on the first Duke of Marlborough in 1705 by Queen Anne, in gratitude for his defeating the French.

The old royal manor house was probably Rosamund's bower, although bower (a reference to the wind) is an old name for a maze and the old tale is that Fair Roz, Henry II's mistress, was kept by the king at the centre of a labyrinth here. His jealous Queen Eleanor found her way to the 'Rose of the World' and forced her rival to drink poison and kill herself. Next to the demolished house was Rosamund's Well, where the king's mis-

Fair Rosamund's well

tress used to bathe. This can still be seen. When the execution of Charles I left the manor house without an owner in 1649, the parliamentary commissioners made the building their base while they surveyed the property. According to legend, they were visited by the devil in the form of a spectral dog. The subsequent nightly noises and visitations may have been either diabolical or the work of Giles Sharp, secretary to the commissioners and a keen Royalist with an ability to make fireworks. Anyway, the frightened commissioners soon packed their bags and left.

The Walk

1. Face the Rose and Crown and go left, soon turning right to take the signposted public footpath through a kissing-gate into Blenheim Park. Go ahead to reach an estate road near a corner of a lake (Queen Pool). Turn right along this for 100 yards. Turn left across the grass just beyond a house, cross a second drive and maintain your direction uphill, passing close to the Column of Victory on your right. Follow a fence on your right to another drive ahead.

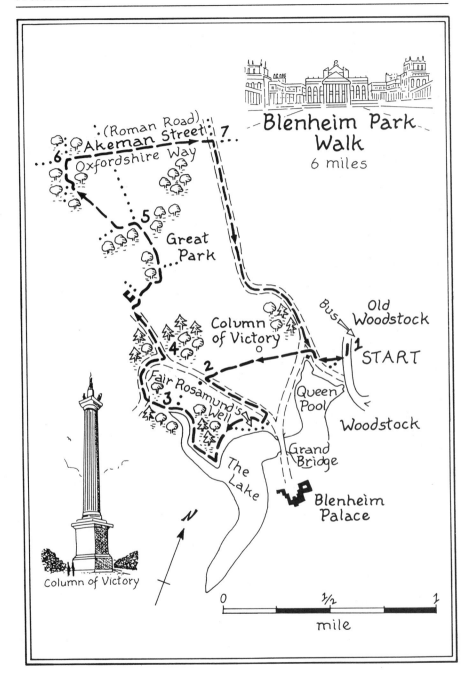

(Roman Road)
Akeman Street 7
6 Oxfordshire Way

Blenheim Park Walk
6 miles

Great Park

5

Column of Victory

Old Woodstock

Bus

1 START

4

Fair Rosamund's Well

2

3

Queen Pool

Woodstock

Column of Victory

The Lake

Grand Bridge

Blenheim Palace

N

0   ½   1
mile

2. Turn left along the drive and approach the Grand Bridge, with Blenheim Palace beyond it. Turn right before the bridge to walk above the lake on your left. The right of way passes above the well associated with Fair Roz and bears right up an arm of the lake.

3. Go ahead, bear left over a stile and skirt the tree-clad slope on your left. Bear right with a drive across a cattle grid and follow it up to a junction.

4. Turn left along the drive to Park Farm. Bear right with the drive to put the farm on your left and, when the drive bears left, leave it at a cattle grid to turn right with a signposted footpath, crossing a stile. Pass a clump of trees on your left and turn left over a waymarked stile to pass a second clump of trees on your left and cross a stile in the fence ahead. Cut across a corner to the stile beside a gate on your right.

5. Enter a new field and turn left, as waymarked, to walk along its left-hand edge. Bear right, as waymarked, at the next fork to cross the field. Turn right for 20 yards at the far end, then take a gap between the trees on your left. Turn right along the track shielded by the trees.

6. Turn right at a crosspaths to follow the waymarked Oxfordshire Way as it runs along the Roman Akeman Street. Go ahead at a crosstracks.

7. Turn right along the drive towards the Column of Victory. Go ahead over a cattle grid and bear left, then right with the drive, which takes you back towards the lake. Retrace your steps by going left back across the grass to the gate out of Blenheim Park and go left for the Rose and Crown.

8. Charlton-on-Otmoor

Route: Islip – Oddington – Charlton-on-Otmoor – Ot Moor – Noke – Islip.

Distance: 9½ miles. Moderate.

Maps: OS Pathfinder 1092 Woodstock, OS Landranger 164 Oxford.

Start: Islip railway station (SP 526145).

Access: Trains run to Islip from Oxford and Bicester. Bus no 94 links both Islip and Charlton-on-Otmoor with Oxford and Bicester (tel. 01865 331249 for details). Telephone 01865 778428 to find out when access is safe through the firing range at direction point 7.

The Goddess and a Garlanded Cross

Ancient customs would survive in a place like Charlton-on-Otmoor. Centuries ago this area of low-lying land was swamp and bog, resting on a layer of clay some 450 feet deep. Ill-drained by the original course of the River Ray, it became a shallow lake in winter and the source of the Christmas goose. The Romans had managed to drive a road through Otmoor, but the land wasn't drained until the 19th century, provoking riots by the dispossessed commoners. Transformed into a pattern of square fields, it may have inspired the chess game in Lewis Carroll's *Through the Looking Glass.*

Our pagan ancestors seem to have made an image of the goddess, using branches and flowers, perhaps to represent the Flower-Woman Blodeuwedd, created by Gwydion to become the wife of Lleu, or perhaps Rhiannon in her role as a fertility goddess. These were paraded at Beltane, May Day. The Roman Catholic Church allowed such customs to continue, but replaced the goddess with a figure of the Virgin Mary. These incurred the wrath of the Puritans at the Reformation. Like other churches, in 1548, St Mary's at Charlton-on-Otmoor lost the figure of the

Virgin Mary that once stood above its fine rood screen. The villagers couldn't forget their old ways, however, so that a tradition survived until today of making a cross out of branches, well 'waisted' to resemble a female figure. Carried in procession through the village on May Day, it is then left on the rood screen until next year's fresh branches. In the first field crossed on the way out of Islip once stood a palace of Ethelred the Unready. King Edward the Confessor was born here in 1004 and baptised in Islip's St Nicholas's Church. Edward the Confessor granted Islip and part of Noke to the Abbey of Westminster, so those inhabitants of Noke ('where nobody spoke') who paid their tithes to Islip

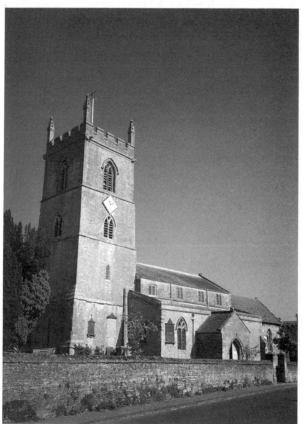

buried their dead there too. Thus the right of way between Noke and Islip became known as a 'coffin' path. Such 'coffin' paths are, by nature, straight, suggesting that they mark leys or spirit paths whose history goes back to the days of Charlton-on-Otmoor's goddess.

NB At direction point 7, this route goes through a firing range; telephone 01865 778428 to find out when access is safe.

St Mary's Church, Charlton-on-Otmoor

The Walk

1. Go up the access lane from the station to Islip and go left along Bletchingdon Road. Go left, then right, in the village. Turn left along North Street. When this bends right, go straight ahead over a stile beside a gate to follow the signposted Oxfordshire Way. Walk beside a hedge on your left, take a waymarked gate ahead and bear left diagonally through a field to cross a stile in its far left corner.

2. Turn right over a bridge and bear slightly left through a gate ahead, aiming for a waymarked stile some 150 yards to the right of the far left corner and the railway. Cross the subsequent footbridge and go ahead through a field to another footbridge 100 yards to the right of a railway crossing in the corner on your left. Bear left in the next field to a stile in the hedge giving access to the railway.

3. Cross the railway carefully and go right to soon find a stile on your left. Bear left over it and along a shaded path. Emerge over a stile and go ahead beside a hedge on your left. Turn right in a corner and follow the hedge on your left to a stile ahead. Cross the railway again and continue over a stile and along the left-hand edge of a field. Cross the footbridge in the corner ahead. Go ahead beside a hedge on your left.

4. Turn left over a stile near the corner and turn right in the next field to walk beside the hedge on your right for 20 yards, then bear right through a gap and bear slightly left ahead through a field to reach a road.

5. Go left along the road to a junction, where you turn right, as signposted for Oddington. Go left at a T-junction to reach Charlton-on-Otmoor and St Mary's Church.

6. Pass The Crown pub and turn right down a track signposted as a bridleway and called Otmoor Lane. Cross a bridge over the New

River Ray, go ahead 300 yards and turn left with the track, ignoring a stile on your right.

7. Turn right at a track junction. This section goes through a firing range. Telephone 01865 778428 to find out when access is safe. Turn right with the hedged track.

8. Do not cross the bridge ahead. Turn left with a track.

9. Turn right over a bridge and along the track ahead. Pass a stile for the signposted Oxfordshire Way on your left as you enter Noke. Pass another signposted path on your left, then a third path on your left and a signposted path on your right, to pass St Giles's Church, Noke, on your right.

10. Turn right with the signposted Oxfordshire Way to follow the 'coffin' path to Islip, bearing right when you reach a road to cross a bridge over the River Ray as you enter the village.

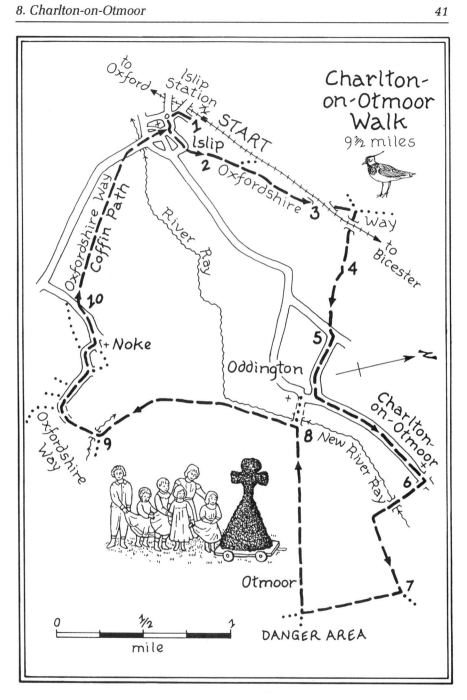

to Oxford
Islip Station
START
Islip

Charlton-on-Otmoor Walk
9½ miles

1

2 Oxfordshire
3

Oxfordshire Way
Coffin Path

River Ray

way
to Bicester

4

10

5

+ Noke

Oddington

N

Charlton-on-Otmoor +

9

Oxfordshire Way

8 New River Ray

6

Otmoor

7

0   ½   1
mile

DANGER AREA

9. Minster Lovell

Route: White Hart, Minster Lovell – Charterville Allotments – Worsham Mill – Minster Lovell Hall – White Hart, Minster Lovell.

Distance: 6½ miles. Moderate.

Maps: OS Pathfinders 1091 Burford & Witney (North) and 1115 Witney (South) & Carterton, OS Landranger 164 Oxford.

Start: The White Hart Inn, Minster Lovell (SP 315110).

Access: Bus no X3 links Minster Lovell with Witney and Oxford, while bus no 102 connects Minster Lovell with Witney and Carterton; telephone 01865 772250 for details.

A Skeleton in a Secret Room

Cast your mind back to those dull history lessons on the Wars of the Roses. You may remember that old piece of doggerel verse:

'The catte, the ratte and Lovell the dogge
Ruleth all England under the Hogge'?

The Hogge was the unfortunate and unpopular King Richard III, who lost his crown and life at the Battle of Bosworth in 1485. His favourites Catesby and Ratcliffe were the catte and the ratte. Lovell was the dogge because a dog featured in his crest (just as a wild boar was included in King Richard's crest). Bosworth was supposed to mark the end of the Middle Ages and the start of the Tudor dynasty, but Francis Lovell didn't realise this from his refuge in Flanders. He fought for the pretender Lambert Simnel and had to go on the run after the Battle of Stoke, near Newark, in 1487. A trusted old servant provided him with food and drink while he survived in a secret room of his hall at Minster Lovell. King Henry VII actually granted the hall with the rest of Lovell's estate to his uncle Jasper Tudor, who is known to have visited it in 1494. By then, however, the hall no doubt had a grisly skeleton in its cupboard, for the old servant must have died, leaving the fugitive to die from hunger and thirst in his place of concealment. Francis Bacon mentioned in his *History of Henry VII* (1622) that Lord Lovell was said to have escaped from the battle at Stoke and survived for a long time in a vault, but the tragic secret wasn't out until 1708, when workmen were laying the foundations for a new chimney in Minster Lovell Hall. They broke into a secret underground chamber and found a man's skeleton seated at a table, equipped with book, pen and paper. The evidence quickly turned to dust.

The Minster part of this place-name was derived from the church (a 'monasterium'). Dedicated to St Kenelm, a Mercian king murdered by his sister in 822, this was rebuilt by the seventh

Baron Lovell when he returned from service in France and decided to settle here in 1431. The church and small priory, dissolved in 1414, that he demolished had been dedicated to St John.

The Charterville Allotments were started by the Chartist leader Feargus O'Connor in 1847. Families arrived from all over England to live off two to four acres of land, a pig and £30 to start off with. The land was soon mostly sold to locals.

Minster Lovell

The Walk

1. Face the White Hart Inn and go left along the pavement of the B4047. Pass a signposted footpath on your left. Turn right to cross the road carefully and go through a waymarked gate. Follow a track to a field, walking with a fence on your left until it turns left, then maintaining your direction ahead through the field, bearing very slightly right to take a gap in the hedge. Continue over a stile and bear left over two more stiles. Take a narrow, fenced, path between gardens (Charterville Allotments).

2. Turn left along a lane for five yards, then turn right between gardens with another narrow path. Emerge over a footbridge and stile in the corner of a field. Go ahead along its left-hand edge, passing a golf course on your left. When the track bears left, turn sharply right through the field with a waymarked bridleway.

3. Bear left over a stile and walk with a hedge on your left. The path, now enclosed by a fence on your right, swings right to run parallel to the A40. Cross Brize Norton Road and continue along the signposted bridleway ahead.

4. Turn right along a lane. Cross the B4047 and take a lane ahead, signposted for Worsham. Cross a bridge over the River Windrush at Worsham Mill.

5. Bear right with the signposted bridleway of a Circular Walk to Minster Lovell. Follow this track to a field and go ahead with a hedge on your right in four fields.

6. Follow the path through a gap in the hedge on your right and as a hedged track past a fifth field on your left. Go ahead beside a hedge on your right in the next three fields.

7. Turn right down a road, climb to a junction and go right. Turn left

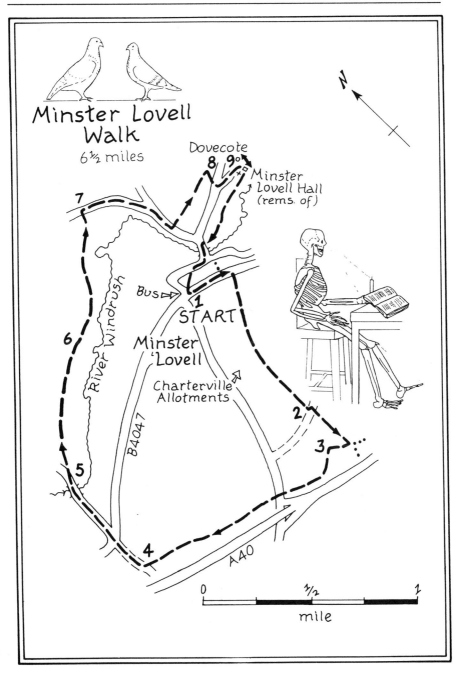

Minster Lovell
Walk
6½ miles

Dovecote

Minster
Lovell Hall
(rems. of)

7

8 9

START

Bus

1

6

River Windrush

Minster
Lovell

Charterville
Allotments

B4047

5

2

3

4

A40

0   ½   1
mile

with a signposted footpath up steps and over a stile. Go ahead along the right-hand edge of two fields. Turn right in a corner to follow the hedge on your left to a road.

8. Turn right along the road to a junction and turn left down the lane to St Kenelm's Church. Enter the churchyard and pass the church on your right to visit the ruins of the hall (now in the care of English Heritage). Take the kissing-gate in the bottom left-hand corner to go left and visit the dovecote.

9. Retrace your steps to the church, pass this on your right and leave the churchyard by a stone stile in the wall ahead. Continue through a meadow, cross a footbridge and a stile in its far left corner, then turn right to walk beside a hedge on your right. Take a stile in the corner and bear left to a stile giving access to playing fields. Cross these to a road, turn left over a bridge and bear right with the road. Go left up steps to take the signposted and enclosed path uphill back to the White Hart Inn.

```
┌─────────────────────────────────────────────┐
│                                               │
│                10. Bladon                     │
│                                               │
└─────────────────────────────────────────────┘
```

Route: Begbroke – Spring Hill – Bladon – Begbroke

Distance: 5½ miles. Moderate.

Maps: OS Pathfinder 1092 Woodstock, OS Landranger 164 Oxford.

Start: The Royal Sun Inn, Begbroke (SP 471139).

Access: Buses to Begbroke include nos 20, 20A, 20B & 20C from Oxford and Chipping Norton. Bladon is served by bus no 42 (Woodstock - Witney). Telephone 01865 772250 for information on these buses.

A Warrior Path

The Column of Victory in Blenheim Park is seen at close quarters in Walk 7 (Woodstock). Erected to commemorate the first Duke of Marlborough's victory over the French in 1704 at the Battle of Blenheim, a ley passes through it, coming south from Ditchley Gate. Crossing the Grand Bridge (near the site of the old royal manor house and Fair Roz's bower), it passes through Blenheim Palace, the birthplace of Sir Winston Churchill, then the grave of Britain's greatest war-lord at Bladon. Appropriately, Bladon's church is dedicated to the warrior-saint Martin. This ley is more than a spirit path, it is a warrior path. Continuing southwards, it clips the edge of the ancient earthworks of Round Castle on Bladon Heath. Leys often clip the edges of hillforts, rather than going through them (cf Walk 4, Chastleton). This warrior path then takes in the summit of Spring Hill before crossing the River Thames or Isis at King's Lock.

Matthew Griffith was the rector at Bladon upon the restoration of King Charles II in 1660. This was his reward for being a staunch Royalist during the Civil War. He proceeded to harangue his congregation from the pulpit so passionately that one Sunday he burst a blood vessel and dropped dead.

The Walk

1. Go west from the roundabout at Begbroke, passing the Royal Sun pub on your left and going up Spring Hill Road. Soon pass the access for St Michael's Church on your right. Pass a signposted footpath on your left. Reach the end of this No Through Road, ignore a signposted bridleway on your left and go ahead up the signposted footpath for Cassington.

2. Follow a farm access track as it bends left to pass woodland on your left. Cross a stile beside a cattle grid and go ahead as waymarked. Pass a house and notice a stile on your left. Turn right through the field to take a gap in the hedge opposite to reach Spring Hill.

3. Turn right to walk beside a hedge on your right in this and the next two fields. Take a footbridge 50 yards to the left of the third corner and continue with a hedge on your left in the next field. Go ahead over a stile to the right of a gate ahead and walk beside a hedge on your left. Continue over a stile and aim for a corner formed by trees jutting into the field ahead. Reach a stile beside a signpost in the far corner, giving access to a road.

4. Turn right along the road for 300 yards, then bear right over a stile and follow the signposted footpath to Bladon, keeping beside a hedge on your left. Cross a stile, go left, bear right in the corner and reach a road. Go ahead at the crossroads and take Church Street to St Martin's Church, Bladon. Pass the church and Sir Winston Churchill's grave on your right. Leave the churchyard by its far gate.

5. Turn right up a lane which soon becomes a path running beside a hedge on your right. When the field on your left ends, turn right to walk beside a hedge on your left. Reach a road.

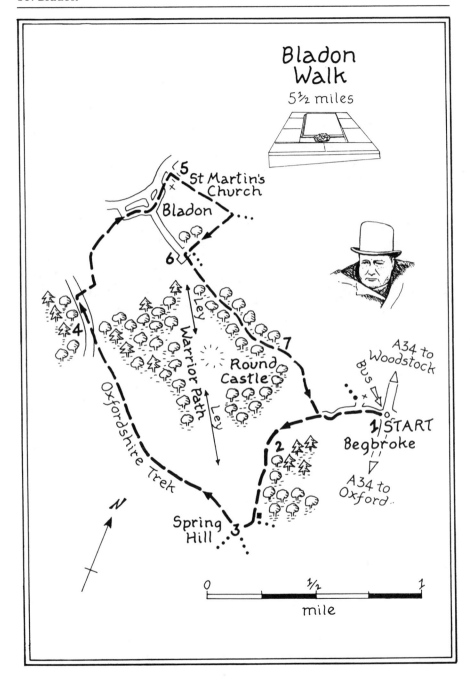

Bladon
Walk
5½ miles

5 St Martin's
Church
Bladon ...

6

4

Ley

Warrior Path

Ley

Oxfordshire Trek

Round
Castle

7

A34 to
Woodstock

Bus

1 START
Begbroke

2

A34 to
Oxford

Spring
Hill 3

N

0   ½   1
mile

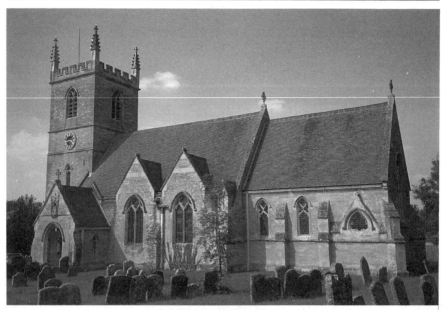

St Martin's Church, Bladon

6. Turn left along the signposted bridleway to Begbroke, soon passing garages on your left, then taking a gate to go along the left side of a long, narrow, field with woodland on your right. Follow the path into the wood at the top end of this field, taking the waymarked gate.

7. Emerge from the wood through the waymarked gate to follow the bridleway along the left-hand edge of a field. Take a gate in the corner and a narrow, enclosed, path to your outward road. Turn left to retrace your steps to the roundabout, the bus stop and the Royal Sun Inn, Begbroke.

11. Godstow

Route: Wolvercote – Godstow – King's Lock – Wytham Great Wood -Wytham Mill – Godstow – Wolvercote.

Distance: 7 miles. Easy.

Maps: OS Pathfinders 1092 Woodstock and 1116 Oxford, OS Landranger 164 Oxford.

Start: Wolvercote bus terminus, Webb's Close (SP 488095).

Access: Buses nos 60 & 60A link Oxford with Wolvercote (tel: 01865 711312 for details).

Fair Rosamund

Rosamund was the daughter of Walter de Clifford. who sent her to Godstow Nunnery to finish her education. Nearby was a high-class brothel in the form of Godstow's Trout Inn, where she caught the eye of King Henry II. The king soon had Fair Roz installed in the royal manor house at Woodstock as his mistress (see Walk 7). The traditional tale is that Henry's queen, Eleanor of Aquitaine, had her rival poisoned, then her body was buried at Godstow. In fact, Rosamund may simply have retired to become a nun at the abbey. In any event, her tomb was there. Royal endowments paid for silken curtains around it and continuous prayers for Rosamund's soul. Bishop Hugh of Lincoln didn't approve of all this in 1191 (two years after Henry II's death) and ordered the remains to be cast out. Upon his departure, the nuns gathered the bones in a bag, however, to be kept in a lead coffin in the Chapter House. When the coffin was opened at the Dissolution, it was found to smell sweetly.

Rosamund bore Henry two sons, William Longspee (Earl of Salisbury) and Geoffrey (who became Lord Chancellor of England). Pilgrims flocked to the shrine of the 'Rose of the World'.

Despite her adultery with the king, she 'had been confident of salvation' and predicted that a tree would turn to stone when it occurred. A tree duly obliged at her death, believed to be in 1176.

The Walk

1. From the bus terminus in Webb's Close, Wolvercote, go right to pass Port Meadow car park and toilets on your left and cross a bridge over a channel of the Thames. Pass the Trout Inn on your left and cross two more bridges over the Thames. Turn left along the Thames Path downstream with the river on your left to see the ruins of Godstow Abbey on your right.

Godstow Abbey

2. Retrace your steps to the road, cross it and continue along the Thames Path, going upstream with the river on your right. Pass under a road bridge and by King's Lock. Take a high gate to walk with Wytham Great Wood on your left and emerge through another gate.

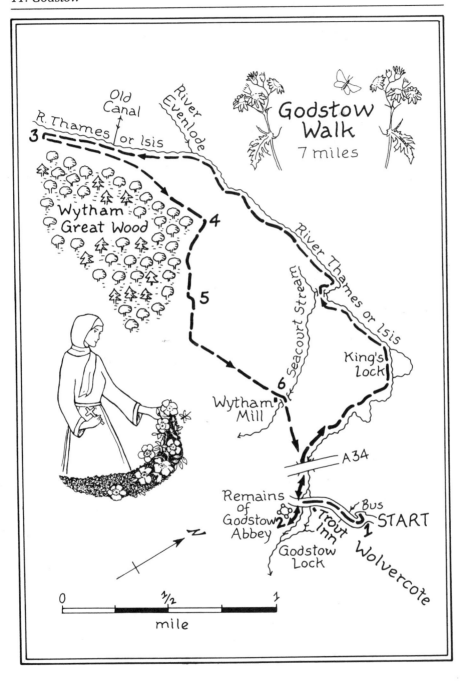

Godstow
Walk
7 miles

3. Turn left for a few yards away from the river and turn left again through another high gate to take a path with a high fence on your right, walking downstream through the fringe of Wytham Great Wood with the river hidden below on your left. Emerge from the wood through another high gate into the corner of a meadow. Go ahead beside the perimeter fence of woodland on your right, gradually diverging from the river.

4. Turn right, as waymarked, to keep the high fence on your right. When you reach a track going away from the wood, turn left along it for about 50 yards.

5. Turn right over a stile to walk with a hedge on your right. Go ahead over a stile and along the top of the next field. Take a gap into the following field and turn left to walk downhill with a hedge on your left. Continue across a track.

6. Pass Wytham Mill, cross a bridge and bear right through a meadow. Continue through the next meadow to rejoin your outward path at the road bridge. Retrace your steps under it and back to the bus terminus at Wolvercote.

12. Stanton Harcourt

Route: Stanton Harcourt – Pinkhill Farm – Pinkhill Lock – Stanton Harcourt.

Distance: 5½ miles. Easy.

Maps: OS Pathfinder 1116 Oxford, OS Landranger 164 Oxford.

Start: The Harcourt Arms, Stanton Harcourt (SP 416057).

Access: Bus no 2 links Stanton Harcourt with Oxford, while bus no 45 comes from Witney. Telephone 01865 883074 for details. There is also bus no 18 (Witney – Oxford) – telephone 01865 772250.

A Fertility Sacrifice?

August 1st is Lughnasadh, a day sacred to the ancient sun-God Lug. This is Llew of the long hand in Leo's month of August. Holding his Lance of Light, he is Sir Lancelot, famous for his strength, courage, constant and too-loving heart. So hot is this sun-God that the earth-mother falls for him and, by his adultery with Guinevere, Lancelot fails the Grail-Quest, brings down the whole Round Table and the Fellowship he held dear. This is the time of harvest, a festival of plenty, when the earth has given birth to its fruits. There is usually a price to be paid, an acknowledgement given by sacrifice. Thus it was on the eve of Lughnasadh, 31st July, 1718, that John Hewet, aged 25, and Sarah Drew, aged 18, farm hand and milkmaid of this parish, sheltered on a haycock as thunder rumbled over-head. The couple were to be married the next week and John was found laying beside Sarah, with his arm outstretched in protection against a flash of lightning. The lovers had been struck to death and were buried together. As it happened, the poet Alexander Pope was staying as a guest of Lord Harcourt in a tower of the manor house (since known as Pope's tower), where he was working on his translation of the *Iliad*. As a result, there is a memorial plaque to the couple above the sun dial (dated 1359) on the outside wall of the south transept of St Michael's Church. It bears an epitaph by Alexander Pope:

'Think not by rigorous judgement seiz'd
A pair so faithful could expire,
Victims so pure Heav'n saw well pleased
And snatched them in celestial fire.
Live well and fear no sudden fate,
When God calls virtue to the grave
Alike 'tis justice soon or late,
Mercy alike to kill or save.
Virtue unmoved can hear the call
And face the Flash that melts the Ball.'

Pope told his friend Lady Mary Wortley about this story, to which she replied:

'Who knows if 'twas not kindly done?
For had they seen the next year's sun
A beaten wife and cuckold swain
Had jointly curs'd the marriage chain.
Now they are happy in their doom
For Pope has wrote upon their tomb.'

Inside the church, look for the remains of the very standard that Sir Robert Harcourt, Standard Bearer to Henry VII, carried at the Battle of Bosworth in 1485 (when Lord Lovell was on the other side, see Walk 9). Look too for the tomb of his grandmother, Lady Margaret Harcourt. Her effigy shows the Order of the Garter with the motto in embossed letters worn above the elbow of the left arm. This tomb became important when Queen Victoria ascended the throne because it been been forgotten by 1837 where a lady should wear the Garter. The Hanoverian kings hadn't invested their consorts with the noble Order, no records bad been left by earlier reigning queens, yet Victoria was to become Sovereign of the Order of the Garter. The church also houses the shrine of St Edburg, brought here by Roman Catholic sympathisers when it would have been destroyed at Bicester at the Reformation. What may be the oldest surviving wooden screen in England divides the Chancel from the Nave. Painted on this is St

St Michael's Church

Etheldreda or Audrey, the seventh century Abbess of Ely from whom we have the word 'tawdry' because she loved cheap jewellery in her youth. The church's dedication to St Michael suggests a link with leys and earth energies, as does the reference to stones in the place-name Stanton. There was a Neolithic stone circle here.

When looking at Pope's tower, you may see the ghost of a Grey Lady. She was Lady Alice, a daughter of the Harcourts who was raped, then murdered by a resident chaplain in his bedchamber. He attempted to hide her body in the fish pond, behind the church, so this is now known as the Lady's Pool.

The Walk

1. Face the Harcourt Arms from across the road, with the church at your back. Go right along the pavement. When the road bears left, go right with a signposted footpath. Pass a playground on your left and continue to reach a road.

2. Turn right along the road to the edge of the village and go ahead with the signposted footpath towards the River Thames. Take a kissing-gate beside a gate and go along the left-hand edge of a field, bearing right near its end to go through a gate to the next

field. Maintain your direction through this and cross a footbridge in its far left corner.

3. Turn right to walk beside a hedge on your right, passing two fields on your left. Turn left at a crosspaths to walk with the hedge on your left. Cross a bridge over a stream and enter the next field. Walk beside a hedge on your right, then follow the waymarked bridleway past Pinkhill Farm and continue along its access lane.

4. Turn right as signposted for the Circular Walk to the towpath and Pink Hill Lock. Beware of adders! Turn right in the corner, as waymarked. Bear left with the hedged path to emerge over a stile beside a gate and go ahead along the left-hand edge of a field. Go ahead across a footbridge and reach the River Thames, on your left.

5. With Pink Hill Lock shielded by trees on your left, cut straight through the meadow ahead to meet the river on your left again and cross a stile ahead. Walk with the river on your left and go over a footbridge to reach the next field. Continue to a waymark post, where you cut diagonally through the meadow to its far right corner.

6. Take the waymarked gate and bear right across a flat concrete bridge, then bear left through a field to a waymarked gate in its far right corner. Go ahead beside a hedge on your right.

7. Turn right over a stile beside a gate in the corner and take the lane ahead back to Stanton Harcourt. Go right to return to the Harcourt Arms, with St Michael's Church on your right.

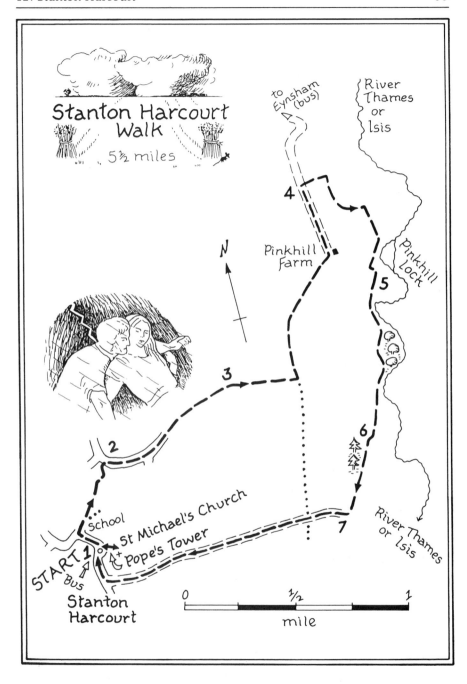

Stanton Harcourt
Walk
5½ miles

to Eynsham (bus)

River Thames or Isis

N

4

Pinkhill Farm

Pinkhill Lock

5

3

6

2

START 1

Bus

school

St Michael's Church

Pope's Tower

7

River Thames or Isis

Stanton Harcourt

0   ½   1

mile

13. Cumnor

Route: Cumnor – Bessels Leigh – Appleton – Bablock Hythe – Cumnor.

Distance: 6½ miles. Easy.

Maps: OS Pathfinder 1116 Oxford, OS Landranger 164 Oxford.

Start: St Michael's Church, Cumnor (SP 461042).

Access: Buses nos 66 & 66A stop at Cumnor on their way between Oxford and Swindon (tel. 01793 428400 and 01793 522243 for details). Buses nos 4A & 4B also link Cumnor with Oxford (tel. 01865 785400).

Dudley's Wife

Nine parsons had to come from Oxford to lay the ghost of Amy Robsart at Cumnor. Amy was the wife of Robert Dudley, the childhood sweetheart of Queen Elizabeth I. She stood in the way of Dudley marrying the queen. Interestingly, Welsh legend affirms that the young Elizabeth did go through some ceremony of betrothal with Dudley and that she secretly gave birth to his son near Llangollen. The boy was brought up as Francis Bacon and was one of the real writers of the plays attributed to William Shakespeare.

Events changed dramatically in the mid-16th century and Elizabeth's accession to the throne in 1558 followed the uncertainties created by her sister Mary's reign, from 1553. The young Dudley had married Amy in 1550, in King Edward VI's short reign, and was imprisoned by Mary for conspiring with his father, the Duke of Northumberland, to make Lady Jane Grey queen. He soon found favour at Elizabeth's court, being appointed Master of the Horse. Amy saw little of her husband and didn't have a home of her own. She stayed at houses of friends and may have been depressed, even suicidal. Whilst staying at Cumnor Place, she died in suspicious circumstances on Sunday, 8th September, 1560. She had sent all her servants to Abingdon Fair for the day. When they returned, Amy was dead. She had ostensibly fallen down the stairs and broken her neck. A full inquiry concluded that her death was accidental. Many were prepared to believe that the ambitious Dudley had his wife strangled and thrown down the stairs. Her husband heard the news at Windsor Castle, where he didn't seem affected by it. He didn't attend his wife's funeral in St Mary's, Oxford. Queen Elizabeth didn't marry him but Dudley was created Earl of Leicester within three years. Sir Walter Scott enlarged upon the story in *Kenilworth*. Cumnor Place, which stood west of the church, was demolished in 1810. Inside the church is a fine statue of Queen Elizabeth I, reputedly erected by Dudley.

The path between Bablock Hythe and Cumnor is an ancient one. A ferry is known to have carried wayfarers across the River Thames here since 904, There was probably a ferry in Roman times (a Roman stone altar has been dredged up). In 1853, Matthew Arnold wrote of the Scholar Gipsy who:

'..at the ferry Oxford riders blithe,
Returning home on summer nights, 'have met
Crossing the stripling Thames at Bablockhythe,
Trailing in the cool stream they fingers wet,
As the punt's rope chops round.'

The Walk

1. With St Michael's Church at your back, go left and soon pass Cumnor's post office on your left. Fork left along Appleton Road. Pass a signposted path and duckpond on your right. As the road bends right, fork left along the drive to the cricket club.

2. Go ahead along the track past the cricket club, on your left. Bear left across a ditch and turn right to follow the ditch on your right southwards.

3. Take a stile in the corner and go ahead with a woodland path to emerge in a field. Go ahead beside a hedge on your right. Take a footbridge in the next corner and bear slightly left through a field, then beside a hedge on your right. Reach a road at Bessels Leigh.

4. Go right with the road to the
    end of the village, then turn
    left along a farm track which
    bends right. Pass barns on
    your right as you continue
    with a grassy track. Take a
    stile into woodland, emerge
    over a footbridge and along
    an enclosed path. Go over a
    stile and through a field to
    St Laurence's Church, Apple-
    ton. Bear right along Church
    Road to the main road
    through Appleton.

5. Go right along the pavement
    to pass the Thatched Tavern
    on your right (although it's
    not   thatched   now!).

Approaching St Laurence's Church

    Go ahead 300 yards from the end of the pavement and the
    Appleton road sign. Turn left with a signposted footpath which is
    a grassy headland track going round the left-hand edge of a field
    and reaching a road at Eaton, leaving the field in its second corner.

6. Go left along the road to Bablock Hythe. Just before the ferry
    across the River Thames, turn right through a gate to follow a
    track signposted as a bridleway to Cumnor.

7. Turn sharply right with the signposted path, passing Leys Cottage
    on your right. Turn left to walk past playing fields on your right. Go
    ahead over a stile, through a field and over another stile. Turn right
    to reach the duckpond passed on your outward journey and bear
    left to retrace your steps to the church.

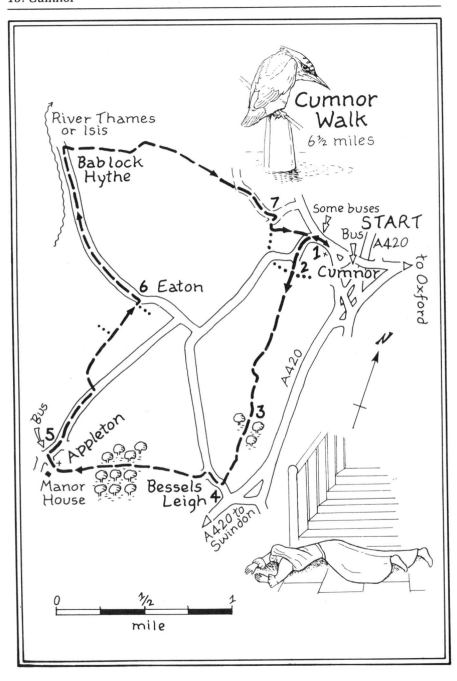

Cumnor Walk
6½ miles

River Thames or Isis

Bablock Hythe

Some buses

START

Bus A420

to Oxford

1

2 Cumnor

6 Eaton

A420

N

3

Bus

5 Appleton

Manor House

Bessels Leigh 4

A420 to Swindon

0   ½   1
mile

14. Oxford

Route: Carfax – St Giles's Church – Radcliffe Camera – Christ Church Meadow – Oxford Castle – Carfax.

Distance: 3 miles. Easy.

Maps: OS Pathfinder 1116 Oxford, OS Landranger 164 Oxford.

Start: Carfax, Oxford (SP 513062).

Access: Oxford can be reached by train and bus directly from many parts of the country.

The Navel of Britain

In the ancient British story of Lludd and Llefelys (and why do schoolchildren in Oxford today know ancient Roman, Greek and Jewish tales, but not their own, just as they learn Latin and Greek, but not Welsh?), Oxford was found to be the navel of Britain. The dragons which feature in that story were caught in a covering of silk draped over a tub of mead in a pit dug at Carfax. They were then taken to Snowdonia, so read more about them in *Walks in Mysterious Wales.* Carfax is where two leys cross, described by Alfred Watkins in *The Old Straight Track.* One runs south from St Giles's Church, through St Mary Magdalen's, St Michael's of the Northgate, St Martin's at Carfax and St Aldate's to Folly Bridge. The other goes east from the site of Osney Abbey through the site of St Peter's in the Castle, St Martin's at Carfax, All Saints' in the High and St Mary the Virgin's.

A third ley may mark the line of the May Day sunrise, going through Christ Church Cathedral and the tower of Magdalen College, where choristers sing in the May Day sunrise and below which Morrismen start their dancing, then to Bury Knowle, Headington.

The Memorial Gardens, Christ Church College

St Frideswide is said to have founded the original religious house on the site of Christ Church Cathedral in AD727. The name meant 'Bond of Peace' in Saxon and she had chosen to be a nun, rather than married to a king.

Oxford is one of those places it would take several lifetimes to acquire a real knowledge of. So many people have been here and so much has happened, it is only practical to dip a tiny pot into its vast ocean and examine a sample of its waters. So, this route is far from comprehensive. It can't even claim to be representative. It does provide sufficient, however. The easiest way of knowing what there is as you walk along is to include details of Oxford's mysteries with the directions, so that you don't have to keep turning pages.

The Walk

1. Face the clock-face of St Martin's tower, Carfax. Across the road to your left is the site of Swindlestock Tavern, where the Town and Gown riots started on St Scholastica's Day, 10th February, 1355.

    Go right to walk up the right-hand side of Cornmarket Street. Almost immediately, stop at no 3. Ask to visit the Painted Room on the second floor. This used to be the Crown Tavern and its 16th century wall-paintings can still be seen. William Shakespeare often stayed here and was godfather to William Davenant, the son of the proprietor John Davenant, in 1606. William Davenant went on to become the first official Poet Laureate, in the reign of King Charles I. Perhaps his talent was inherited, because 'tis said that William Shakespeare was his real father. As to whether William Shakespeare wrote all or any part of the plays attributed to him, that's another matter.

    Continue northwards (with the ley) to St Michael's of the North-gate, on your right. Climb its tower to check the line of the ley running south from St Giles' and to see an ancient fertility carving known as a Shiel-na-gig. Kept in a display case and of pagan Celtic origin, this is a woman exposing and accentuating her genital area. Brides used to acknowledge it before entering the church.

    Continue past St Mary Magdalen's on your right, cross the road at the traffic lights on your left to continue up the ley by passing the Ashmolean Museum on your left and walking up the left-hand side of St Giles. This broad street has a ghostly place-memory of King Charles I reviewing his troops here during the Civil War, when Oxford became his temporary capital − 'city of dreaming spires and lost causes'.

2. Turn right at the pelican crossing at the foot of Woodstock Road

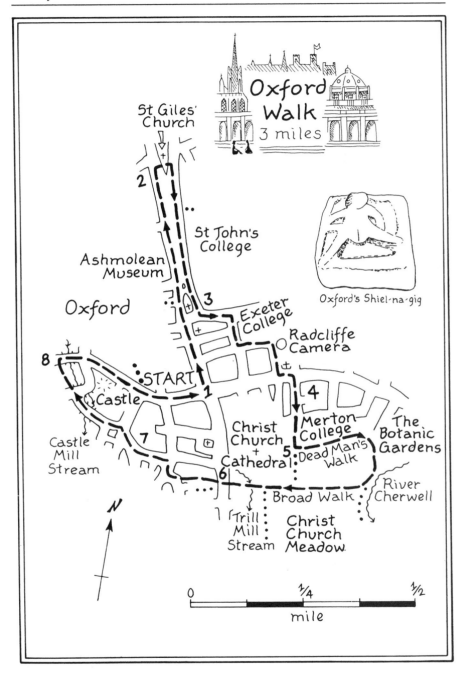

St Giles'
Church

Oxford
Walk
3 miles

Oxford's Shiel-na-gig

2

St John's
College

Ashmolean
Museum

Oxford

3

Exeter
College

Radcliffe
Camera

8

START

1

Castle

4

Castle
Mill
Stream

7

Christ
Church
+
Cathedral

Merton
College

5 Dead Man's
Walk

The
Botanic
Gardens

6

Broad Walk

River
Cherwell

Trill
Mill
Stream

Christ
Church
Meadow

N

0   ¼   ½

mile

and take the path ahead past St Giles' Church on your left. The ghost of a grey lady is said to haunt this churchyard. Cross the pelican crossing at the foot of the Banbury Road and turn right to return down the other side of St Giles. Pass St John's College on your left. William Laud was its President before becoming King Charles I's outspoken Archbishop of Canterbury. Executed in 1645, his tomb is before the altar of St John's College Chapel. When your author was a chorister here, he was regaled with tales of Laud's ghost bowling its head along the ground in the college library. Pass the Martyrs' Memorial on your right.

3. Turn left at Broad Street. Balliol College is on your left and in the middle of the street is a cross set in the surface to mark the spot where the Protestant Bishops Latimer and Ridley in 1555 and, in 1556, Archbishop Crammer were burned at the stake in the reign of Bloody Mary. They are commemorated by the Martyrs' Memorial at the southern end of St Giles. Turn right along Turl Street to pass Exeter College on your left. The resident headless ghost here also wears 17th century dress and is believed to be John Crocker, whose statue is in the college chapel. Turn left along Brasenose Lane to the Radcliffe Camera. Go right to pass St Mary the Virgin's on your left and reach the High. Go left to a pelican crossing, take it and go right for 10 yards. The timbered house now owned by Barclay's Bank at the corner of Magpie Lane and the High has the ghost of a young Puritan lady who fell in love with a dashing young cavalier during the Civil War. When her lover didn't return, she died of a broken-heart.

4. Turn left along Magpie Lane. Cross Merton Street to pass Merton College on your left. Merton is the college with the oldest statute, being officially founded in 1274. Its Mob Quad was built between 1304 and 1378, while its library claims to be the oldest in England. The ghost of Sir Thomas Bodley can be seen in Tudor costume in this library, which must have inspired him to found the Bodleian Library in 1602. Enter Christ Church Meadows.

5. Go left along Dean Man's Walk, below the walls of Merton College. This route earned its name when Jewish funeral processions took it to their burial ground at the site of the Botanic Garden. The name was apt when Colonel Windebank was executed here during the Civil War. This Royalist officer was shot for failing to do his duty when he surrendered Bletchingdon House to Oliver Cromwell. His ghost may be seen on Merton College's wall. As you approach the eastern end of Dead Man's Walk, look for a plaque in the wall commemorating the first English balloon trip, made by James Sadler on October 4th, 1784. He landed near Woodeaton. Turn right in the corner to pass the Botanic Garden on your left and come to the River Cherwell. Turn right along Broad Walk and continue across the culverted Trill Mill Stream, explored by T.E. Lawrence (of Arabia) when he was a student at Jesus College. Leave by the gates of the Memorial Gardens to go ahead across St Aldate's.

6. Go ahead along Rose Place. Turn right at Littlegate Street and turn left at Turn Again Lane. Pass Pike Terrace on your left and come to the end of houses on your right.

7. Here, on your right, was King's Terrace. When your author lived at no 3 (now demolished) as a child and was born here, there was a plaque stating that this was the approximate site of the grave of Roger Bacon, who died in 1292. Read more about this greatest of Oxford's earlier scholars in Walk 17 (Sunningwell). After the demolition of much of St Ebbe's and the erection of the Westgate shopping centre, the plaque was put back in the wrong place and can be seen on the wall about 100 yards ahead and on your right. Go ahead along Old Greyfriars Street and bear right across Castle Street to take Paradise Street. Cross the Castle Mill Stream and pass Oxford Castle on your right. Empress Matilda escaped from King Stephen's siege by riding down the frozen Thames from here to Wallingford in December, 1142. Go ahead past

St Thomas' Street on your left and Tidmarsh Lane across the bridge on your right. Walk with the stream on your right to reach Park End Street.

8. Turn right across a bridge, pass Tidmarsh Lane on your right and go up New Road, passing Nuffield College on your left. Notice Oxford Castle Mound on your right. This is where Mary Blandy of Henley-on-Thames (see Walk 27) was executed. Her ghost has been seen here. Continue through Bonn Square, passing Westgate Shopping Centre on your right. Follow Queen Street back to Carfax.

15. Shotover

Route: Thornhill Park & Ride – Shotover Plain – Country Park – Thornhill Park & Ride.

Distance: 3½ miles. Strenuous.

Maps: OS Pathfinder 1116 Oxford, OS Landranger 164 Oxford.

Start: Thornhill Park & Ride (SP 564074).

Access: As well as the Thornhill Park & Ride bus from Oxford, there is a bus stop near the start of this walk for the X90 bus (London-Oxford) and bus no 280 (Aylesbury – Oxford). Bus no 22 serves the nearby Risinghurst estate from the centre of Oxford (tel. 01865 711312 for details).

A Lost Giant

According to the Book of Genesis, 'there were giants in the earth in those days'. It has been suggested that thousands of years ago the earth was slightly closer to the sun, making the year a perfect 360 days and, for some reason that a NASA scientist could fathom, our planet's gravity different enough for giants (and huge reptiles, known as dinosaurs) to exist. Something nudged us into our present orbit and the giants died out. Certainly, there is plenty of evidence for them in legend and, indeed, some giant bones. The last of the really big giants of Albion was said to be Gogmagog, who was hurled to his death by Corineus, a follower of Brutus, who renamed the land Britain around 1100 BC. A skeleton of a male giant 8ft 6ins (2.6m) tall was unearthed on the Isle of Lundy in 1850, next to a 7ft 8ins (2.3m) female skeleton. These bones may have dated from AD 450. It seems that our ancestors revered the dead bodies of the giants so much that they were placed on hillsides and their outlines traced in the turf, as happened to Gogmagog on Plymouth Hoe and may have been the origin of the Cerne Abbas giant.

The old coach road

The red soil of Shotover Hill once sported the outline of a giant, known in the 17th century as Sir Harry Bath, Bear or Barkley. He reputedly shot his arrow over the hill (hence the name – and a folk memory of a ley?). The effigy has long been overgrown and lost. A circle that may have formed the giant's face did show up on an infra-red photograph taken from the air in 1968. This was on the slope above Brasenose Wood (above direction point 6 in this walk). In 1723, the giant was said to be near the third milestone east from the city of Oxford. The old stage-coach route to London ran over Shotover Plain and the third milestone was probably near where you emerge at direction point 3.

The Walk

1. From the southern side of the A40 just west of Thornhill Park & Ride, near Nielson House, go south along the signposted public footpath to Shotover Plain, taking a gate and going ahead along an enclosed path. Emerge in the corner of a playing field and go ahead along its left-hand edge.

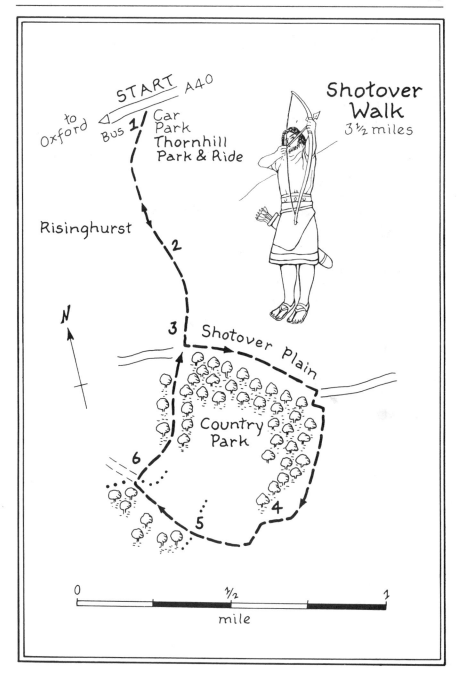

START A40

to Oxford

Bus **1**/ Car
Park
Thornhill
Park & Ride

Risinghurst

Shotover
Walk
3½ miles

N

2

3 Shotover Plain

Country
Park

6

5

4

0   ½   1

mile

2. Cross a footbridge and stile in the far left corner and continue along a narrow, fenced, path. Climb to a stile and signpost on Shotover Plain.

3. Turn left along the broad track of the old stage-coach road. Take a gap in the trees on your right and soon turn left when waymarked by a blue arrow. Walk inside woodland, with a field on your left. Bear right at a fork, as waymarked by a blue arrow. Descend to gain a view over Oxford and bear right.

4. Take the left fork ahead, as waymarked, and follow a board-walk which bears left. Cross a footbridge, go left then bear right along the foot of a field. Go through a gap in the corner and along the foot of the next field.

5. Go ahead at a waymarked path junction in a wooded area, ignoring the bridleway going left. Cross a lane and take the woodland path ahead.

6. Emerge at a junction with a lane. Turn right with a path waymarked by blue arrows. Climb back up (passing the lost giant on your left?) to Shotover Plain and go ahead across it to retrace your steps to the start.

16. Bampton

Route: The Horseshoe Inn, Bampton – Primrose Lane – The Plantation – St Mary's Church, Bampton – The Horseshoe Inn, Bampton.

Distance: 3½ miles. Easy.

Maps: OS Pathfinder 1115 Witney (South) & Carterton, OS Landranger 164 Oxford.

Start: The Horseshoe Inn, Bampton (SP 314031).

Access: Bus no 19 connects Bampton with Witney and Carterton (tel. 01865 772250 for details).

The Morrismen

Bampton may be a small and remote place now, but it was once an important market town with an annual horse fair, suggesting a link with the goddess Rhiannon. It is still famous for its morris dancing. Records show that the Morrismen have danced every Whitsun or Spring Bank Holiday in Bampton since at least the 14th century, if not from the beginning of human history in this part of the world. While a fiddler plays, eight Morrismen dance the old dances in the presence of a 'Fool' or clown. A swordbearer carries a cake in a round tin impaled on his blade, decorated with ribbons, so that women bystanders can eat a portion and gain fertility. This tradition must be a reminder of pagan fertility rites, while the dancing involves much stamping upon Mother Earth, as if she likes a good massage. The Morrismen are a mystery, as befits their appearance with blackened faces hidden behind brightly-coloured streamers. The name may be derived from Moorish and there may be a connection with the East, even with those legendary Phoenicians who involved themselves in our prehistory. The sword would suggest ancient sacrificial rites. The original link was probably with May Day (Beltane). This is the place to come on Spring Bank Holiday!

The Walk

1. With your back to The Horseshoe Inn, cross the road and take the lane signposted as a public footpath ahead. Bear right along an enclosed path and walk beside a wall on your right. Cross a footbridge and go right along a track known as Primrose Lane. Turn right at Weald Street to reach the A4095. Go left along the pavement for 150 yards.

2. Bear right over a stile to follow a signposted path which passes Ham Court and the remains of a castle built by the Earl of Pembroke around 1315 away to your right. Go ahead over a footbridge and bear left beside a stream on your left. Bear right to cross a stile in the fence ahead. continue over another stile and

walk beside a hedge on your right. When this ends, join the track running parallel on your right, then bear slightly left through a field to a footbridge. Cross this and emerge at the edge of a field.

3. Go right, with the belt of trees on your right. Look out for a waymark post on your right and bear right when indicated through the plantation of trees. Emerge over a stile in the corner of a field. Go ahead and bear right to a brook. Turn left across a footbridge and bear right

The footbridge crossed at point 3

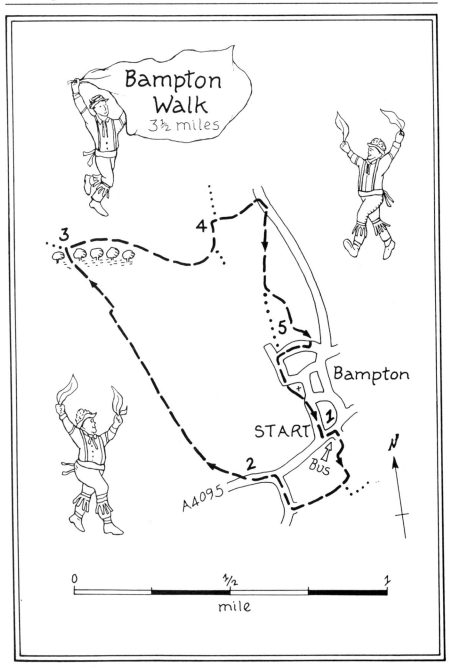

through the next field to a waymark post at a corner formed by hedges. Continue beside a hedge on your left and take a stile in the corner ahead.

4. Turn right to walk with a hedge on your right. Turn right at a road for 100 yards. Bear right through a gate to take the signposted footpath towards Bampton's church spire. Go ahead over a stile in the far hedge and walk beside a hedge on your right.

5. Take the stile to the left of a wall ahead and go left to reach a kissing-gate beside a gate. Take this to gain access to a lane. Go right to pass a cemetery on your right and bear left to the church. Take the path through the churchyard, passing St Mary's Church on your left. Go right along Church View and turn left at the end to return to the bus stop and The Horseshoe Inn.

17. Sunningwell

Route: Radley station – Radley Park – Sunningwell – The Fox – Jarn Mound – Boars Hill – Bayworth – Kennington – Radley station.

Distance: 9 miles. Strenuous.

Maps: OS Pathfinders 1116 Oxford and 1136 Abingdon, OS Landranger 164 Oxford.

Start: Radley railway station (SU 526989).

Access: Trains run to Radley from Oxford and London Paddington. Buses nos 30 (tel. 01865 727000), 35 & 35A (tel. 01865 785400) run through Radley on their way between Oxford and Abingdon.

A Wonderful Doctor

Roger Bacon was the greatest of Oxford University's scholars in the Middle Ages. Known as Dr Mirabilis (wonderful doctor), he was a Franciscan, a philosopher and a scientist. The subjects he studied and contributed to included theology, astronomy, astrology, medicine, optics, mathematics and alchemy. His religious superiors feared heresy and kept him locked up for most of the 1280s, when he would have been in his sixties. His study was on Folly Bridge, on an island between two channels of the Thames. He loved to come to Sunningwell to study the

Sunningwell Church

stars, however, taking his astrolabe up to the top of the church tower. He gained a reputation as a magician and was believed to have been in contact with the souls of the dead. His own death probably came in 1292 and he was buried at the Franciscan House in Oxford (see Walk 14, point 7).

Roger Bacon wouldn't have recognised St Leonard's Church's seven-sided porch. This was a present from Bishop Jewel of Salisbury, Sunningwell's rector, in 1551. Jewel was a Protestant who fled to Germany in 1555 when Mary acceded to the throne. He returned with the accession of Elizabeth I to be consecrated Bishop of Salisbury. He died in 1571. Another famous incumbent was Dr Samuel Fell, who became Dean of Christ Church College, Oxford. A fervent Royalist, he died of a broken heart at the news of Charles I's execution. Before that he had been evicted from the university for being a Royalist. When the Chancellor of Oxford, the Earl of Pembroke, came to evict him, he told Pembroke that 'he was too inconsiderable a person to parley with'. The outraged earl sent Fell to prison and turned his family out of the Deanery. The outspoken Dr Fell had himself threatened to send down an undergraduate from Christ Church. He gave the student one chance, however, to immediately translate from the Latin Martial's epigram on Sabidius, the literal translation of which is 'I do not love thee, Sabidius, nor can I say why. I can only say this, I do not love thee'. The student translated:

'I do not love thee, Dr Fell,
The reason why, I cannot tell;
But this I know, and know full well, I do not love thee, Dr Fell.'

Matthew Arnold found inspiration in the Boars Hill area for his *Thyrsis* and *The Scholar Gipsy*. Speculative builders threatened to ruin the area in the 1920s, but the views were safeguarded by the formation of the Oxford Preservation Trust which purchased the land in 1928. Sir Arthur Evans, the excavator of Knossos, erected a mound on Jarn Heath, now known as Jarn Mound. A lover of 'antiquity, nature, freedom and youth' for 'all to enjoy', he employed unemployed Welsh miners during the Depression and made a wild garden. Trees now obscure the view from Jarn

Mound, which has a toposcope. Did Sir Arthur know that Jarn Mound is on leys or spirit paths? The most important goes to Pope's Tower, Stanton Harcourt (Walk 12), another goes either to Carfax or Oxford cathedral (Walk 14), while a third links Jarn Mound with Roger Bacon's observatory at Sunningwell church.

The Walk

1. From Radley station, go right along Foxborough Road and pass St James's Church on your right. Turn right along Kennington Road and soon turn left at the main entrance to Radley College, forking right to take the drive lined by chestnut trees. Pass the cricket ground, where Ted Dexter once played, on your right.

2. Leave the drive as it turns right and go ahead through parkland, passing a lake on your left. Follow an avenue of trees and take a series of gates to reach the A4183 road.

3. Cross the road and bear left along a private road but public path. Continue over a stile beside a gate and bear left with the path as it prepares to cross the A34 by a bridge. Cross this bridge and turn left down steps to take a fieldpath to Sunningwell, where St Leonard's Church is on your right.

4. With the church on your right and before the duck pond on your left, turn left uphill along a signposted footpath. Go ahead through a gate and along a road until a turning on your left marked for Broomwood, The Croft and Ashbrook. The road bears slightly right here. Go straight ahead along a narrow footpath to emerge opposite a pub called The Fox. Cross the road and go left along the pavement for 30 yards.

5. Turn right with the signposted footpath to walk along the right-hand edges of two fields. Halfway along the top of the second field, turn right with a narrow path into the woods. Emerge at a stony lane, soon becoming metalled as it joins a lane, where you turn right and go ahead to Jarn Mound. Climb the steps to the toposcope at the top, then descend and take the path which passes Jarn Mound on your right and comes to a road.

6. Turn right along the road and go ahead at a crossroads to take the pavement of Berkeley Road. At the next T-junction, on Boars Hill, turn right along the pavement of Foxcombe Road.

7. Turn left down Lincombe Lane (signposted as a public footpath). When this lane bends right, go straight ahead over a waymarked stile to take a shaded path. Follow it around to the left and cross a stile to go down the left-hand side of a field. Go over a stile in the corner and take a footbridge at the bottom of the next field to walk past chalets and reach a lane.

8. Go right along the lane. When it turns right, go left with a track and soon bear right to cross a stile beside a signpost. Go ahead along the left-hand edge of a field, cross a footbridge and a stile and maintain your direction through a golf course. An enclosed path leads to a road at a junction. Cross it to take the road ahead, signposted for Kennington (Bagley Wood Road). Cross a bridge over the A34.

9. Reach a junction with St Swithun's Road and turn right along a signposted footpath, soon forking right with a hedged path that emerges in the corner of a sports field. Continue along the right-hand edge of this and the next field. Go ahead over a stile and a footbridge to walk with woodland on your left, keeping just inside the wood. Emerge at a road and cross it to maintain your direction along a fieldpath. Come to more woodland on your left.

10. Bear left through a waymarked gate and soon go right with a delightful path which skirts Radley College's playing fields. Take waymarked gates ahead and turn left to reach the road near a bus stop. Go right, then left, to return to the railway station.

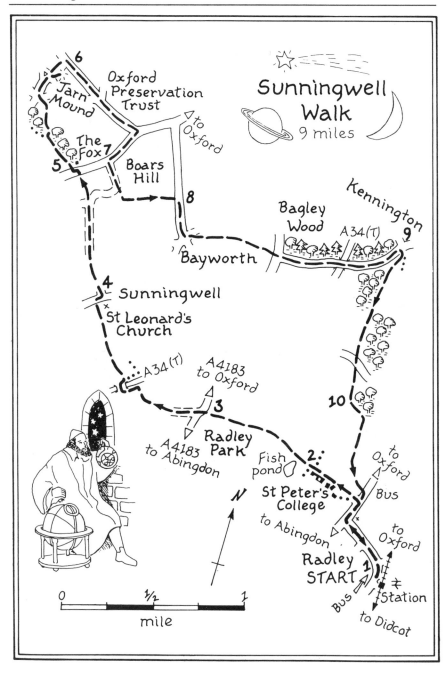

Sunningwell Walk
9 miles

6
Jarn Mound
Oxford Preservation Trust
to Oxford
The Fox 7
5
Boars Hill
8
Bagley Wood
A34(T)
Kennington
9
Bayworth
4 Sunningwell
St Leonard's Church
A34(T)
A4183 to Oxford
3
Radley Park
A4183 to Abingdon
Fish pond
2
10
to Oxford
Bus
St Peter's College
to Abingdon
to Oxford
Radley START 1
Bus
Station
to Didcot

N

0   ½   1
mile

18. Garsington

Route: Plough Inn, Garsington – Southend – The Platt – Denton – St Mary's Church, Garsington – Plough Inn, Garsington.

Distance: 3½ miles. Moderate.

Maps: OS Pathfinder 1116 Oxford, OS Landranger 164 Oxford.

Start: The Plough Inn, Garsington (SP 580022).

Access: Bus no 101 links Garsington with Oxford and Watlington (tel: 01865 772250 for details).

The Michael Current

One of the most remarkable alignments of ancient sites runs from west Cornwall to east Norfolk via such places as Glastonbury Tor and Avebury. Followed by Hamish Miller and Paul Broadburst, it is described in their book *The Sun and the Serpent*. They found that the straight ley was accompanied by winding Michael and Mary (male and female) energy currents. Garsington's hilltop church is dedicated to St Mary, but the Michael current runs through it. Cuddesdon is its immediate destination to the east, while it goes to Clifton Hampden (Walk 20) via St Peter's at Marsh Baldon in the west. It can be dowsed, while the church stands on the obvious site, commanding the highest viewpoint (nearly 400ft – 121m – high) between Oxford and the Chilterns. Its position is the essence of the village, whose name means 'grassy hill' (Gaerse dun). The church contains a memorial by Eric Gill to Lady Ottoline Morrell, the brewer's wife whose home in Garsington's Manor House became a sanctuary for such artists and intellectuals as Aldous Huxley, Bertrand Russell, Virginia Woolf, D.H. Lawrence, Maynard Keynes and Siegfried Sassoon during the difficult days of the first world war. Riger Haggard, the author, also lived in Garsington in his youth and used the surname of a local farmer for his hero Allan Quartermain.

Near the Manor House and on the opposite site of the road is an old granary, raised on saddle-stones to discourage rats trying to reach the grain. As you proceed from the Manor House to the church, look for the Gizzel on your left. This pond used to provide the village with water. It is fed by a spring and the old English word 'gysel' means 'gushing'. A Roman sword was discovered in the garden of the Plough Inn.

St Mary's Church, Garsington

The Walk

1. With your back to the Plough Inn, go right down Pettiwell. Come to a footpath signpost and turn left across the road to take the path to St Mary's Church.

2. When level with the church porch, ignore the first path running downhill on your right, but fork right down the next path. Take steps down to a stream.

3. Emerge over a stile and bear left, as waymarked, to walk with a hedge on your left and an orchard behind a wooden fence on your right. Go ahead over a stile beside a gate and bear slightly right through a field to reach a road at a signpost. Go right along its pavement for 50 yards.

4. Turn left along a signposted bridleway along the left-hand edge of a field. Bear left through a gap to continue beside a fence on your right. Return through another gap to the left-hand edge of the initial field and go right to its far corner.

5. Take a gap in the corner and walk parallel to the hedge on your right. Go through a waymarked gate into the next field. Bear left to its bottom left corner and take a hedged path to a road. Go left, ignore a lane on your right, then take the road for Garsington on your left.

6. Bear left over a stile beside a gate to take the signposted path through four fields to Garsington. Turn right up the road to pass the Gizzel and the church on your left on your way back to the Plough Inn.

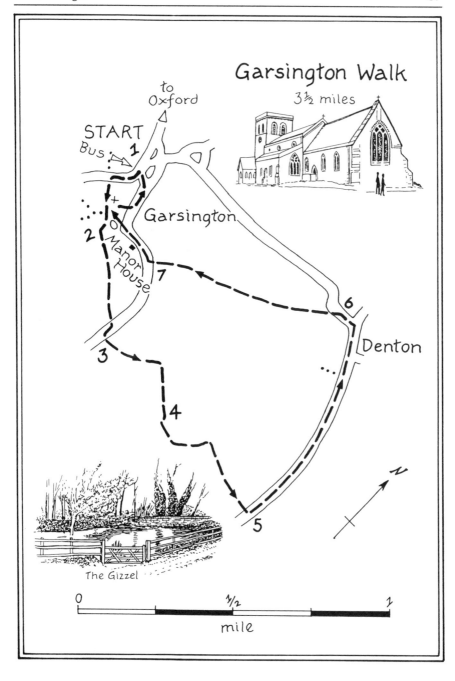

to Oxford

START

Bus **1**

Garsington Walk

3½ miles

Garsington

Manor House

2

7

6

Denton

3

4

5

N

The Gizzel

0   ½   1

mile

```
┌─────────────────────────────────────────────────────────────┐
│                                                               │
│                    19. Faringdon                             │
│                                                               │
└─────────────────────────────────────────────────────────────┘
```

Route: Faringdon – Littleworth – Tagdown Barn – Folly – Faringdon.

Distance: 5½ miles. Moderate.

Maps: OS Pathfinder 1135 Faringdon, OS Landrangers 163 Cheltenham & Cirencester and 164 Oxford.

Start: The Bell Hotel, Faringdon (SU 289955).

Access: Buses nos 66 & 66A link Faringdon with Oxford and Swindon (tel. 01793 428400 and 01793 522243 for details).

A Folly on a Hill

Follies abound in the English countryside, substantiating the claim that we are a nation of eccentrics. But is there a method in our madness? Do we, either consciously or unconsciously, erect monuments precisely where they are needed? The folly on Faringdon Hill, for instance, marks the ley from Rollright stone circle (Walk 3) to Uffington white horse (Walk 23). This virtually north-south ley can be dowsed going through the folly, as can an east-west ley (linking, perhaps, with the Dragon line across southern Britain at Clifton Hampden – see Walk 20). Curiously, the hill acquired its name before its actual folly. This is a brick tower 104 feet high. It was erected in 1935 by Lord Berners to give work to the local unemployed and as a birthday gift for Robert Heber-Percy (who later inherited Faringdon House). Locals complained vigorously against it, with one old soldier's reference to 'Lord Berners' monstrous erection' perhaps an allusion to the lord's notoriously unmarried condition. Real men, like one old admiral, railed against him and objected to it receiving planning permission.

When it was finally opened on 5th November, 1935, hundreds of doves dyed red, white and blue were released. Lord Berners left a note reading 'Members of the public committing suicide from this tower do so at their own risk'. The trees around the folly were planted by Henry Pye, who was King George III's Poet Laureate. His poems helped to drive the King mad and lose us the American colonies. He wrote a poem about the view from Folly Hill, entitled 'Faringdon Hill', but it is too turgid to reproduce. A castle existed for a time on Folly Hill, but King Stephen (who fought Empress Matilda) demolished it in 1144. Faringdon means 'fern-covered hill', so this hill was probably always the focus of local attention. It occupies a strategic position between the

Downs and the Thames, which attracted the Saxons. King Alfred had a royal manor here and his son Edward the Elder died in Faringdon in 924. The path used by this route as it leaves Faringdon, passing Church Path Farm, marks the line of another ley or spirit path. Looking back along it towards the church, note that the spire was destroyed in 1645 when Roundheads besieged Royalists here. Actually, it was a Parliamentarian son shooting at his Cavalier father in the manor house. The Pye family conducts its quarrels in style!

The Folly, Farringdon Hill

The Walk

1. With your back to the Bell Hotel, go ahead to the church. Turn right with Church Street. Pass the A4095 going to Witney on your left. When the street turns right, go straight ahead along a stony track signposted as the Circular Walk Footpath to Thrupp. Pass Church Path Farm on your right and continue along a narrow, waymarked, path.

2. Go ahead over stiles at a path junction to continue in the same direction. Pass Haremoor Farm on your right. Soon cross a stile beside a signpost to walk with the fence on your left, then go ahead through an open field to take a signposted gap in a fence ahead. Continue to reach a road at Littleworth.

3. Go right with the road through Littleworth to pass the church on your left and bear right to the A420. Go left along this road's pavement for 200 yards, then turn right across the road and take a firm track between fields, signposted as a public footpath. Keep beside a hedge on your left and turn left with it for 30 yards, then turn right with the track between fields to Tagdown Barn.

4. Turn right to follow a track through a field, going parallel to woodland on your left. Continue with a hedge on your right in the next field. At the end of this hedge, bear right through a gate at a path junction to walk through a field passing Wadley Manor away to your right. Cross a track, take a gate into the next field and go ahead through the right-hand of two gates to the right of woodland.

5. Go ahead along the left-hand edge of a field. Cross the A420 and follow the signposted path up to the tree-covered hill surmounted by the folly. Continue down a metalled path into Faringdon. Reach Stanford Road and turn right with a causewayed path to the main road. Turn left to return to the Bell Inn.

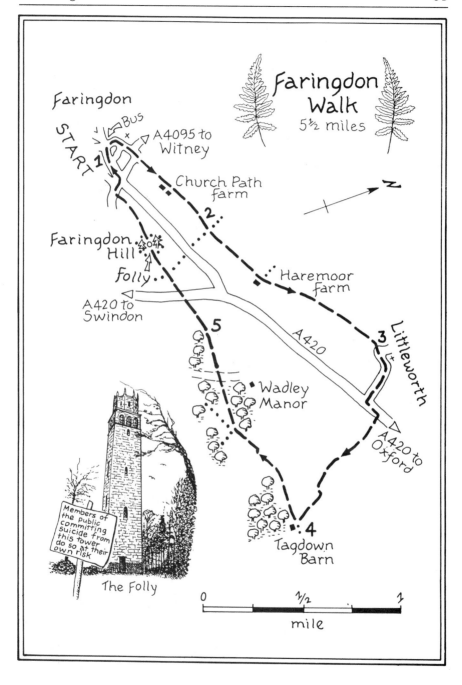

Faringdon

Faringdon Walk
5½ miles

START
Bus
x
↗ A4095 to Witney
Church Path Farm

2

Faringdon Hill
Folly
A420 to Swindon

Haremoor Farm

5

A420

3 Littleworth

Wadley Manor

A420 to Oxford

4 Tagdown Barn

Members of the public committing suicide from this tower do so at their own risk

The Folly

0   ½   1
mile

20. Clifton Hampden

Route: Dorchester — Wittenham Clumps — Clifton Hampden — Dorchester.

Distance: 11 miles. Strenuous.

Maps: OS Pathfinder 1136 Abingdon, OS Landranger 164 Oxford.

Start: Fleur de Lys Inn, Dorchester (SU 579942).

Access: Bus no 390 (tel. 01865 727000 for details) links Dorchester with Oxford and London, while bus no 105 (tel. 01734 583747 or 01734 594000 for details) goes through Dorchester on its way between Oxford and Reading.

The Dragon Line

The dragon represents the currents of earth energy, transmuted by the sword of St Michael, or the Will, into a radiant Light, spreading the Spirit throughout the land. Ancient sites linked with dragons and St Michael align to form a great spirit path across southern England, marking the Beltane (May Day) sunrise. Life-giving energy flows along this line, bringing health and fertility. John Michell wrote about this in *The New View Over Atlantis*, but Hamish Miller and Paul Broadhurst have since devoted their *book The Sun and the Serpent* to investigating and describing it. It crosses the River Thames or Isis at Clifton Hampden, visiting St Michael's Church on its mound above the river.

This little bit of Oxfordshire is one of the most sacred spots in England. Dorchester has an unbroken history of being a town since prehistory, with the Saxons taking over from the Romans who took over from the Ancient Britons. An important neolithic sacred complex is now lost where flooded gravel pits line the road north of Dorchester. It comprised a cursus and big rings. Radio-

On Wittenham Clumps

carbon analysis has dated these to 3000 BC. Castle Hill on Wittenham Clumps has a folk memory of buried treasure guarded by a phantom raven in its eastern ditch (known as the 'Money Pit'). At 403ft (122m) Harp Hill is slightly higher than its neighbour and is an excellent viewpoint, provided with a toposcope.

The earthworks known as the Dyke Hills, on the other side of the river below Wittenham Clumps, defended an important trading centre when the Romans arrived. The Roman town built next to this survived until well after the withdrawal of the legions in AD 410. The Saxons took it over as a going concern and the mysterious Wessex dynasty (the Saxon leaders with British names) received the papal envoy Birinus here in 635. Christianity was already old in Britain and the name Wessex is derived from Gewisse, which could refer to Gnostics rather than West Saxons. However, the baptism of King Cynegils here by St Birinus was highly significant. This ancestor of King Alfred the Great granted land to Birinus in Dorchester for the establishment of a cathedral church and an episcopal see.

Dorchester was an odd choice for such an important function. It was too far north and this proximity to Mercia led to the bishopric being moved to Winchester. That's why, at the end of a long tale, there is only an abbey church here now (but well worth a visit, if only to see the Jesse window). Something was

known about this place by the wise men who arranged such
things as royal baptisms and cathedral sites. The ancient name
of our premier river may provide a clue. The Romans latinized
the British name for the river to 'Tamesis'. Early Saxon records
have variants such as 'Thamisal. The waterman poet John Taylor
wrote a verse about Dorchester in 1632:

'There Tame and Isis doth
embrace and kisse,
Both joyn'd in one, calld Tame
or Tame Isis'.

Here we have it, if we would only look at the earth through the
eyes of our ancient ancestors, who respected it as a living being.
The river now commonly known as the Thames between its
source (disputed, but officially near Kemble, in Gloucestershire)
and Dorchester is actually the Isis. A few people in Oxford
remembered this and braved the scorn of those who scoff at such
things, by perpetuating the name on the Ordnance Survey maps
and in the title of Oxford University Boat Club's second eight. Isis
is the Mistress of the Pyramids. It is recorded that they were
dedicated to this goddess of magic in 10450 BC (cf Graham
Hancock's *Fingerprints of the Gods*). Isis is associated with Sirius
and was particularly remembered for being strong of tongue. She
was renowned for her skilful use of witchcraft and magic. Osiris
was her brother and husband. They mated in the womb of their
mother, the sky goddess Nut. Their son was Horus, who later
became the instrument of revenge on his uncle Set. While Osiris
was away, Set plotted to rule in his stead. On his return, Osiris
was chopped into 14 pieces by Set. These were retrieved by Isis,
with the exception of his genitals. Possessor of the Ankh (symbol
of divine authority and key to the house of life), Isis is represented
by a throne in Egyptian hieroglyphs. The pharaohs were established on her throne, which shows her to be the power of the
earth.

The cult of Isis declined only in name when Christianity was
made the state religion of Rome. Her worship was transferred to
the Blessed Virgin Mary. The statues of Isis suckling Horus

became the models for the Madonna and Child. Mary inherited the role of Bride of God from Isis, while Isis' opposition to Set became Mary's opposition to Satan.

The River Isis is joined by the River Thame just south of Dorchester and below Castle Hill. When their waters mingle, they form the River Thames, or Thamesis (Thame-Isis). Thame is the male counterpart of the divine Wisdom of Isis. One function of Isis is to re-assemble lost knowledge. King Cynegils of Wessex was baptised where the confluence of the male River Thame and the female River Isis form the River Thames, as if mirroring the significance of the sacred grove or clump of trees on Castle Hill. Miller and Broadhurst describe in *The Sun and the Serpent* how male and female 'Michael' and 'Mary' energy lines associated with the dragon line that goes through Clifton Hampden cross in the sacred grove on Castle Hill, above the confluence of the Thame and Isis. Many have been inspired by Wittenham Clumps and the view from them.

Look on the last tree on your right as you go eastwards through the clump on Castle Hill. You can still make out some words of a poem carved on it in 1847 by a member of the Tubb family:

'As up the hill with labouring steps we tread.
Where the twin clumps their sheltering branches spread,
The summit gained, at ease reclining stay,
And all around the wide-spread scene survey.
Point out each object, and instructive tell
The various changes that the land befell.
Where the low banks the country wide surround
The ancient earthwork formed old Mercia's bound.
In misty distance see the furrow heave
There lies forgotten lonely Gwichelm's grave.
Around the hill the ruthless Danes entrenched
And the fair plains with gory slaughter drenched.
While at our feet where stands that stately tower
In days gone by up rose Roman power.
And yonder there, where Thames, smooth waters glide,
In later days appeared monastic pride.
Within that field where lies the grazing herd

High walls were crumbled, stone coffins disinterred.
Such, in the course of time, is the wreck which fate
And awful doom award the earthly great'.

Visit the Pendon Museum (tel. 01865 407365) to see models of the Vale of the White Horse.

The Walk

1. With your back to the Fleur De Lys Inn, Dorchester, go right along the main road to pass the bus stop and reach a telephone box. Fork right down Bridge End, passing a car park, toilets and the Roman Catholic church of St Birinus on your left. Turn right and almost immediately turn left along Wittenham Lane, signposted as the path to the river. Continue along the left-hand edge of a field. When the Dyke Hills are reached and the track turns right to run alongside their earthworks, go straight ahead over a stile. Pass an old pill box on your left and go ahead over a second stile. Reach the confluence of the Thame (on your left) and Isis (ahead), marked by a footbridge on your left (don't cross it!).

2. Turn right to walk upstream with the Isis on your left. Take a bridge over the river, just before Day's Lock. Continue over two more bridges to emerge on a lane. Go ahead to reach St Peter's Church, Little Wittenham, on your right.

3. Turn left into the nature reserve and take the path up the right-hand edge of the field towards Harp Hill or Round Hill (same hill, different names) at Wittenham Clumps. Climb to the toposcope and go clockwise around the clump of trees at the summit. Head for the next clump, on Castle Hill, crossing a track and passing a gate on your left. Cross a stile, follow the path through Castle Hill's ramparts and into the trees at the summit. Bear left at a path junction to see the poem tree, a big tree on your right as this path emerges from the clump. Retrace your

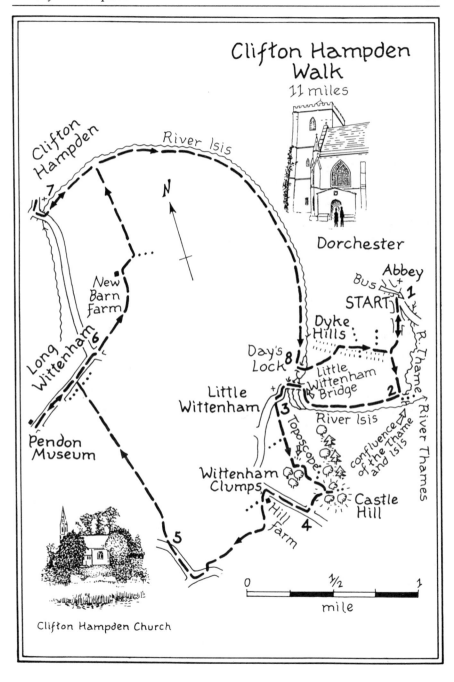

Clifton Hampden Walk

11 miles

Clifton Hampden

River Isis

N

Dorchester

Abbey

Bus

START

1

Dyke Hills

Day's Lock

8

Little Wittenham Bridge

2

New Barn Farm

Long Wittenham

6

Pendon Museum

Little Wittenham

3

River Isis

Toposcope

confluence of the Thame and Isis

R. Thame / River Thames

Wittenham Clumps

Castle Hill

4

Hill Farm

5

0   ½   1

mile

Clifton Hampden Church

steps to the junction in the middle of the sacred grove and fork left to descend to a car park and road.

4. Go right along the road and approach the road sign for Little Wittenham. Turn left along a lane, signposted as a public footpath and with a stile to the left of a gate across it. Pass Hill Farm on your left, ignore a concrete lane which bears right and take the grassy track ahead. Walk with a fence on your right, go ahead over a stile and continue with a fence on your left. Take another stile and go along the left-hand edge of a field. Turn left when indicated by a yellow arrow to reach a road. Go right along the road and turn right, as signposted for Wittenham.

5. As the road bears left, fork right off it, crossing a stile to go along a signposted footpath beside a hedge on your right. Continue over a series of stiles to reach Long Wittenham. Go left through the village to find the Pendon Museum on your right. Retrace your steps and continue to the other end of the village.

6. As the road to Clifton Hampden bears left, fork right and very soon turn left up a No Through Road. Pass New Barn Farm on your left, bear right with the lane and, as it bears right again, turn left along a hedged, grassy track. This leads to the Isis. Go left upstream with the river on your right. Turn right with the bridge across it to Clifton Hampden and visit St Michael's Church.

7. Retrace your steps across Clifton Hampden bridge and go left to walk downstream with the river on your left.

8. Turn left to cross the river at Day's Lock and bear slightly left through a meadow to take a small gate and go ahead along an enclosed path to the Dyke Hills. Turn right to walk to the end of the earthworks and go left to retrace your outward path back into Dorchester.

21. Watlington

Route: Watlington – The Ridgeway Path – Watlington Hill – Christmas Common – Watlington.

Distance: 5½ miles. Strenuous.

Maps: OS Explorer 3 Chiltern Hills South or OS Pathfinder 1137 Watlington & Stokenchurch, OS Landranger 175 Reading & Windsor.

Start: Black Horse Cottage, Watlington (SU 688946).

Access: Bus no 101 comes to Watlington from Oxford (tel. 01865 772250 for details). Bus MI connects Watlington with High Wycombe, tel. 01296 613831. Buses nos 122, 123 & 124 link Watlington with Thame and Henley-on-Thames, tel. 01296 399500.

The Black Horsemen

In the sixth century, King Arthur's knights patrolled the border between Celts and Saxons. This was quite complicated in Oxfordshire, with the Celts retaining the higher ground, such as the Chilterns, while the Saxons had established themselves in the Thames Valley. In *The Black Horsemen*, S.G. Wildman has shown how the Arthurian border can be traced with the aid of old pub names. Where Arthur's knights watered their horses and, no doubt, partook of liquid refreshment themselves, there are found pubs named The Black Horse. Watlington, at the foot of the Chilterns and near the Icknield Way (now forming part of the Ridgeway Path), had such a pub until recently. No 2 Chapel Street was pointed out to me as the former Black Horse pub, while next door is a thatched cottage still named after the black horse.

Christmas Common probably earned its name when the Royalists and Roundheads squaring up to each other on this section of the Chilterns declared a truce on Christmas Day, 1643. I can't see Cromwell's men celebrating Christmas ... no doubt somebody produced a football.

The Walk

1. The former Black Horse pub at no 2 Chapel Street, next door to Black Horse Cottage, is just across the road from the bus stop and public library. With your back to the library, go left and bear right along Chapel Street to pass the former pub on your right and come to the cottage. Return to the public library, face it and go left then almost immediately right along Davenport Place (signposted as a public footpath). Reach a road and turn right along its pavement for 50 yards. Turn left up a narrow,

Black Horse Cottage

   waymarked, footpath. Emerge over a stile and bear right to a stile in the hedge opposite. Cross it and fork left along an enclosed path.

2. Join a firm track and bear left with it. Go ahead across a track coming from your left over a cattle grid. Continue along the left-hand edge of a field. Follow a grassy track as it turns right, then turn left along the right-hand edge of a field, walking parallel to a concrete lane on the other side of the hedge. Take a stile in the corner ahead to reach the Ridgeway Trail (here using the old Icknield Way).

START
The Black
Horse

Bus

1

Watlington

Watlington
Walk
5½ miles

2

6

The Ridgeway Path

The Ridgeway Path

The

3

4

Watlington
Hill

Pyrton
Hill

Car Park

Oxfordshire Way

Christmas
Common

5

N

0   ½   1
mile

3. Turn left along the Ridgeway Trail. There is a permissive footpath on the other side of the hedge on your right as an alternative to the metalled lane. Turn right along the road signposted for Nettlebed. After 400 yards, bear left up a stony lane and soon fork left along the path waymarked as W7.

4. Climb with a hedged path. Reach a road near a car park. Go right to a road junction at Christmas Common.

5. Turn sharply left along the road signposted for Stokenchurch. Soon bear left with the signposted Oxfordshire Way, crossing a stile and going along the left-hand edge of a field. Take a stile in the corner and leave the Oxfordshire way as it bears right through the following field. Instead walk beside the hedge on your left. Bear left over a stile along the path waymarked as W4. Descend through the left-hand edge of woodland and with a view over Watlington opening up before you. Bear right at a waymarked fork (white arrows on a tree) to emerge on the Ridgeway Trail.

6. Turn left along the Ridgeway to a road. Turn right along its pavement to return to Watlington.

22. Wayland's Smithy

Route: Ashbury – Odstone Coombes – Wayland's Smithy – Odstone Down – Ashdown Farm – Alfred's Castle – Ashbury.

Distance: 7½ miles. Strenuous.

Maps: OS Pathfinder 1154 Lambourn Downs, OS Landranger 174 Newbury & Wantage.

Start: The Rose & Crown, Ashbury (SU 265851).

Access: Buses nos 47 & 47A run to Ashbury from Swindon (tel. 01793 428400 for details). The Ridgeway Explorer runs here from Swindon, Wantage and Reading on Sundays and Bank Holidays from May to October (tel. 01865 772250).

Wayland the Blacksmith

'You must tie your horse to that upright stone that has a ring in it and then you must whistle three times and lay down your money on a flat stone and then sit down among the bushes and not look for ten minutes. Then you will hear the hammer clink. Then say your prayers and you will find your money gone and your horse shod'. So wrote Sir Walter Scott in *Kenilworth*, referring to Wayland's Smithy. In Norse mythology, Wayland is a smith of supernatural skill. He was captured by a king and made lame to prevent escape. Set to work, the smith gained revenge by killing the king's two young sons and making cups from their skulls. He then raped the king's daughter and escaped by magically flying through the air. Wayland is actually better known for making gold cups than shoeing horses. Does a gold cup represent the Holy Grail? Above all he was a magician. The tale of paying for a service that is done in secret is a theme well-known to children (cf 'The Elves and the Shoemaker'). Some say Wayland was an elf. As a blacksmith, was he responsible for hammering souls into shape on his forge?

Wayland's Smithy

To archaeologists Wayland's Smithy is two successive neolithic long barrows, built one over the other. It is an impressive sight at nearly 200 feet long and 50 feet wide and has 10 feet high sarsen stones at its mouth. It also dates back to 3700 BC and was enlarged by 3400 BC. Fourteen skeletons were found in the original barrow and eight more in the extension.

Wayland's Smithy lies beside the Ridgeway. This official National Trail was opened as an 85 mile route between Overton Hill and Ivinghoe Bacon in 1973. The ancient Ridgeway can be traced for some 300 miles between Devon and Norfolk. An unofficial long distance path of 64 miles now terminates at Wayland's Smithy. It crosses Oxfordshire from Wormleighton Reservoir on the Oxford Canal and is named the d'Arcy Dalton Way after a man who gave 50 years service to the cause of rights of way in Oxfordshire.

The word 'sarsen' for the large stones at the mouth of Wayland's Smith may be derived from Saracen, like 'morris' dancing may refer to Moorish. Is there a message here about people coming from the Middle East in ancient times and teaching old dances and erecting these stones? More sarsens can be seen recumbent near Ashdown House. This land once belonged to Glastonbury Abbey, which is an interesting connection. The 17th century house is now owned by the National Trust. The nearby Alfred's Castle is so-named because King Alfred the Great defeated the Danes on these Downs in 871. The earthwork is prehistoric, however. It was originally faced with sarsen stones.

The Walk

1. With your back to the Rose and Crown, go downhill along the road signposted for the school and Shrivenham. Turn right at Manor Farm, cross the B4000 road and take the signposted metalled bridleway ahead, passing Ashbury Evangelical Free Church on your right. Ignore a signposted path on your right as you descend to a duckpond. Turn right at a lane junction to pass Kingstone Farm on your right and bear right at the fork where the lane joins the B4507.

2. Go ahead along a signposted footpath, crossing a stile and going round the foot of a slope on your left. Bear left to walk with a fence on your right, cross two stiles ahead and go up Odstone Coombes to join a track near trees above the top right-hand corner of the coombe.

3. Turn right along the track to reach the Ridgeway. Turn left along this and soon turn left again to visit Wayland's Smithy.

4. Retrace your steps to the crosstracks where you first joined the Ridgeway and turn left along the track past Odstone Barn to Odstone Down, where you bear right.

5. Pass beyond the far end of the belt of trees on your right, cross

a stile beside a signpost and bear right down to another stile beside a signpost at a road junction.

6. Cross the B4000 to take the road ahead, passing Ashdown Farm on your left and the entrance to Ashdown House on your right. When the lane bears left, turn right along a footpath which follows the right-hand edge of a field. Keep right at a fork and continue over a stile beside a gate to reach the earthworks of Alfred's Castle on your left.

7. Go ahead over another stile beside a gate and walk with woodland on your right. Take a stile beside a gate in the neck of the field and maintain your direction to reach the Ridgeway.

8. Cross the Ridgeway and take the path straight ahead which goes over the brow of the hill and descends to Ashbury. Fork left to pass the church on your right and emerge with the Rose and Crown and the bus shelter on your right.

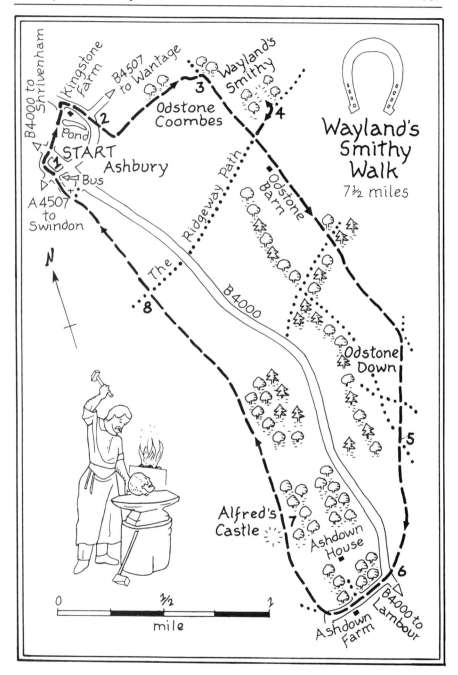

Wayland's
Smithy
Walk
7½ miles

23. White Horse Hill

Route: Woolstone Hill car park – White Horse Hill – The Ridgeway – Whit Coombe – Woolstone Down – White Horse Hill – Woolstone Hill car park.

Distance: 7 miles. Strenuous.

Maps: OS Pathfinder 1154 Lambourn Downs, OS Landranger 174 Newbury & Wantage.

Start: Woolstone Hill car park (SU 293866).

Access: This is the only route whose start I reached by car! I am seduced now and again, I'm afraid – this time by the car-driving Penny Allen. Normally, I would start this walk from the bus stop at the turning for Woolstone on the B4507. Bus no 47A runs here from Swindon on Saturdays (tel. 01793 428400 for times). There is also the Ridgeway Explorer bus on Sundays and Bank Holidays only from May to October. This runs between Reading and Swindon and connects with buses from and to Oxford at Wantage. Telephone 01865 772250 for details.

The White Horse (or Dragon)

Walk here as a pilgrim, for this is holy ground. As G.K. Chesterton wrote in his *Ballad of the White Horse*:

'Before the gods that made the gods, Had seen their sunrise pass, The White Horse of the White Horse Vale, Was cut out of the grass.'

Linked by a spirit path with the Rollright stone circle (Walk 3), this beast is best seen from the air, or at least several miles away in the valley. This prompts thoughts as to who was meant to see it and how did they manage to cut it so accurately? Cut it they did, and scour it every seven years to maintain its outline in the chalk.

Thomas Hughes wrote of the last traditional scouring, in 1857. There were great festivities, including cheese-rolling down the Manger. Now in the care of English Heritage, it is 360 feet long and 160 feet high. Iron Age currency bars link it with the Dobunni tribe. Perhaps it was their tribal badge, aimed to impress those stuck in the valley. They would have been precious few because the Romans were probably the first to tackle the dense forests of the clay vale. The Britons preferred the chalk hills, where the prehistoric Ridgeway ran, with the Icknield Way providing a parallel fine-weather route at the foot of the chalk linking the spring-line villages on a narrow band of greensand. The White Horse stood more chance of impressing a Martian in a flying saucer than people on the Icknield Way. It is there because it is there. It has probably been there for aeons, adopted by successive invaders (if the original population ever were removed). It may not be a horse. It may be a dragon. It could well be both.

Guy Underwood, the dowser, wrote in *Pattern of the Past* that there were two figures – a dragon and a horse. A horse would be appropriate for the Celtic goddess Rhiannon, representing the fertility of the land. Dragons personify the life force, especially when it needs to be controlled by a dragon-slayer. Who better than St George? The seemingly artificial mound below the horse or dragon is called Dragon Hill. This is where George slew the dragon. There are a couple of bald patches on the hill's flat top to prove it. These are bare of grass (and were in previous centuries, according to old pictures). They were scorched by the dragon's blood. Guy Underwood (op. cit.) dowsed blind springs marking terminations of right-handed multiple spirals – 'a phenomenon of great rarity and sanctity'. Read, too, *The Light in Britain* by Grace Cooke. Kenneth Grahame set his story *The Reluctant Dragon* here. Of course, nowadays we must echo John Aubrey's words of 1687:

'To save a mayd St George the dragon slew -
A pretty tale, if all is told be true.
Most say there are no dragons, and 'tis sayd
There was no George, pray God there was a mayd.

There is another ley, according to Paul Devereux and Ian Thomson in *The Ley Hunter's Companion*. Running for nearly 10 miles from Berkshire, it links the site of a tumulus (now ploughed out) near direction point 3 on this walk, Uffington Castle, Dragon Hill

Standing in the eye of Uffington White Horse

and St Mary's Church, Uffington. Dowse this as it crosses your path. Admire one of the finest views in England from a height of 855 feet and stand in the eye of the horse, shut your eyes, turn round three times in a clockwise direction and make a wish. Guy Underwood found a powerful blind spring at this spot too! It traditionally brings good luck.

The Walk

1. Take the gate at the back of the Woolstone Hill car park and go ahead towards the white horse hill figure. The car park just below Uffington Castle is for the disabled and elderly only. Go right from the white horse to walk with the ramparts of Uffington castle on your right and go through a gate to reach the Ridgeway.

2. Turn right along the Ridgeway and walk past Uffington Castle on your right. Ignore the first path running south on your left. Turn left along the second path running south, at a signposted cross-

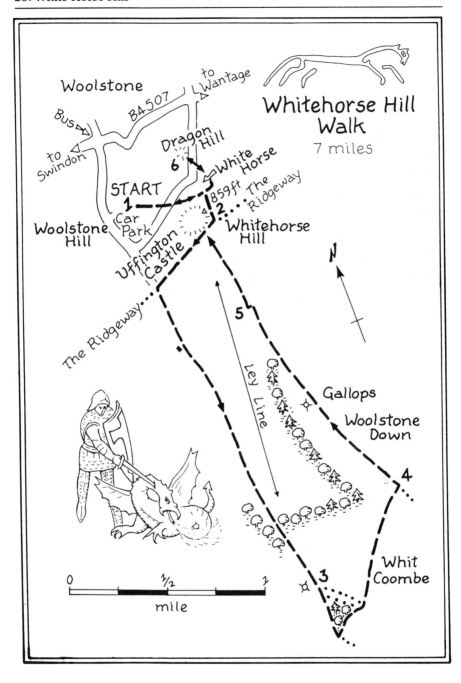

Woolstone

to Wantage

B4507

Bus

to Swindon

Dragon Hill

START

6

1

Car Park

Woolstone Hill

Uffington Castle

White Horse

859ft

2

The Ridgeway

Whitehorse Hill

Whitehorse Hill Walk

7 miles

N

The Ridgeway

5

Ley Line

Gallops

Woolstone Down

4

3

Whit Coombe

0   ½   1

mile

tracks. Follow this track past buildings on your right and past wide acres of ploughed downland, then through a belt of beech trees. A ley running south from St Mary's Church, Uffington and Dragon Hill soon crosses the track and goes through the site of a tumulus in the field on your right (the tumulus has been destroyed by ploughing).

3. Ignore inviting paths which fork left. Bear slightly right with the main track to pass a patch of woodland on your left. Turn left after this woodland and follow the grassy track up Whit Coombe.

4. Turn left at the signpost on the ridge and follow the waymarked path beside the Gallops on Woolstone Down. Pass the end of a belt of trees leading off to your left. Go ahead through a gateway waymarked with blue arrows for a bridleway and turn left.

5. Turn right in the corner to follow the bridleway to the Ridgeway. Go right along the Ridgeway for a few yards before retracing your steps through the gate on your left to pass the ramparts of Uffington Castle on your left and reach the white horse. Pass above the hill figure and descend to cross a road and climb up the mound known as Dragon Hill.

6. Retrace your steps to the white horse and from there to the car park.

24. Wantage

Route: Wantage – Icknield Way – West Lockinge – The Ridgeway – Monument of Lord Wantage – Lark Hill – Wantage.

Distance: 9 miles. Strenuous.

Maps: OS Pathfinders 1154 Lambourn Downs and 1155 Harwell, OS Landranger 174 Newbury & Wantage.

Start: King Alfred's statue, Wantage (SU 398879).

Access: There is an excellent bus service between Oxford and Wantage, including no X3l. The Ridgeway Explorer comes on Sundays and Bank Holidays from May to October. Telephone 01865 772250 for details.

A Statue and a Memorial Cross

Wantage is an ancient place, beside the Icknield Way and below the Ridgeway. The Romans settled here, while the Saxons chose it as a royal manor. Our greatest Saxon, King Alfred, was born here in 849, the fourth son of Ethelwulf, King of Wessex. When they celebrated the millenium of his birth here, a statue was commissioned. This was eventually erected in the market square in 1877 and bore a marked resemblance to Lord Wantage, Colonel Robert Lloyd-Lindsay VC KCB. Its inscription reads:

'Alfred found learning dead, and he restored it:
Education neglected, and he revived it:
The laws powerless, and he gave them force:
The Church debased, and he raised it:
The land ravaged by a fearful enemy, from which he delivered it.'

Robert Lloyd-Lindsay, Baron Wantage, won his Victoria Cross in the Crimean War. When he married Lord Overstone's daughter she brought him the largest estate of Berkshire (to which this part of Oxfordshire belonged until 1974), exceeding 20,000 acres.

They became model estate owners. His widow had a cross erected as a memorial to him in 1901.

As it happens, this cross marks the junction of two leys and stands on an ancient tumulus beside the Ridgeway. Did somebody choose this spot knowing this?

The Walk

1. Face King Alfred's statue and go ahead, passing it on your right. Go ahead along Wallingford Street. Pass Ormond Road on your right and take Charlton Road ahead. Pass Fyfield Close on your right.

2. Turn right up Lark Hill. Turn left with the signposted right of way which follows the route of the ancient Icknield Way. This begins as a track but narrows to a hedged path. Go ahead when you reach a road and bear right with it.

3. Fork right before the road bends left. Take a bridleway from West Lockinge, passing stables on your left. Keep climbing to pass practice jumps for racehorses and come to a hedge ahead.

4. Turn left and walk beside a hedge on your right. Go ahead over a lane and take a waymarked bridleway past woodland. Join a path coming up from your left to continue above more trees on your left and climb past Grim's Ditch to the Ridgeway.

5. Go right along the signposted Ridgeway to overlook Oxfordshire on your right. Pass the memorial cross to Lord Wantage on your left.

6. Approaching a road, turn right through a small metal gate to descend with a signposted bridleway to a similar gate in the lower fence at point 4. Retrace your steps downhill and past the

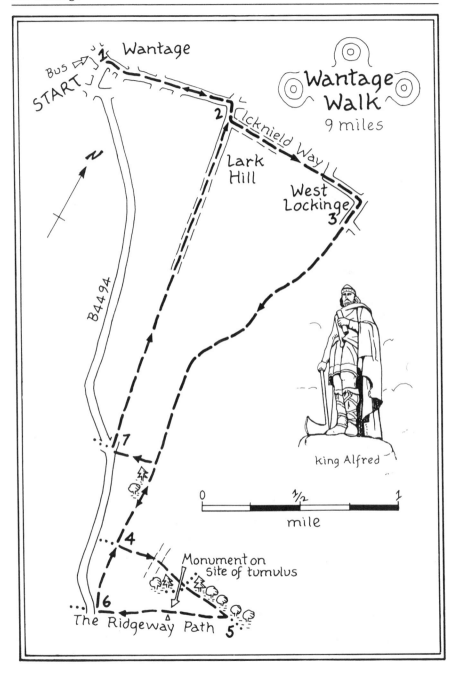

Wantage

Bus
START

Wantage
Walk
9 miles

N

B4494

Icknield Way

Lark
Hill

West
Lockinge

king Alfred

0   ½   1
mile

Monument on
site of tumulus

The Ridgeway Path

plantation of trees on your left. Turn left at the next track junction to walk beside a hedge on your left and reach a road.

7. Turn right along a broad track which becomes the metalled lane at Lark Hill taken for a while by your outward route. Pass the Icknield Way on your right and retrace your steps into Wantage.

King Alfred the Great's statue at Wantage

25. Blewbury

Route: Blewbury — Blewburton Hillfort — Blewbury — Churn Farm — Churn Knob — Blewbury.

Distance: 8½ miles. Strenuous.

Maps: OS Pathfinder 1155 Harwell, OS Landranger 174 Newbury & Wantage.

Start: The Red Lion Inn, Blewbury (SU 530857).

Access: Didcot, with its railway station providing frequent train services to Oxford, is only 3 miles to the north, so if you rely on public transport, allow plenty of time for a 15 mile ramble. There is a bus from and to Didcot on Fridays (tel. 01491 680354).

Churn Knob

The Ancient Britons occupied the hillfort of Blewburton, which was probably destroyed by the Romans when they invaded. The Saxons seem to have moved the settlement to Blewbury and it soon became the most important place for some miles around. An estimated population of 400 in 1086 compares with a population of 623 recorded by the 1851 census. The thatched walls lining the initial path of this walk are reputedly Saxon. The Saxons were converted to Christianity by St Birinus (see Walk 20 about his baptising the King of Wessex at Dorchester). The saint is said to have preached his first sermon on Churn Knob. Dowsing reveals four leys crossing at this ancient mound. One runs from north to south (4 degrees minus 4 for magnetic variation), another at 44 degrees (48-4), a third at 96 degrees (100-4) and a fourth at 116 degrees (120-4). This is clearly a place of great spiritual power and the obvious place to preach from. Hamish Miller and Paul Broadhurst, authors of *The Sun and the Serpent*, find that their Michael energy line goes through both Blewburton Hillfort and Churn Knob.

The Walk

1. With your back to the Red Lion, go left and take the path with the thatched walls in the corner. This leads to the church, which is passed on your right. Go right along a path beside a stream. Go left at a lane junction along South Street. Ignore a lane on your right and come to where Berry Lane goes left and Bridus Way goes right. Go left along Berry Lane for just 10 yards.

2. Turn right along a signposted path. Continue across a footbridge and bear left to take another footbridge. Go ahead along the left-hand edge of a field. Cross a stile in the corner and maintain your direction to a stile in the fence opposite. Cross it and bear right to reach a road junction.

3. Cross the B4016 and go ahead along the road signposted for Aston Upthorpe. Turn right over a stile to walk with a hedge on your left towards the earthworks of Blewburton Hillfort. Turn left over a stile into the hillfort and go right with a fence on your right and the ramparts of the hillfort on your left.

4. Take the stile near the corner ahead and turn right along a track towards Blewbury. Cross the B4016 and go ahead along Bessel-slea Road. When level with Brides Way on your right, turn left along an enclosed path. Turn right at a road for 50 yards, then turn left with a metalled track which soon bears right to become stony. Ignore the first signposted footpath on your left and pass a hedged track on your left.

5. Turn left up a signposted path (choosing between a high or a low level to begin with). Pass a wooded basin on your left, then look out for Churn Knob away to your right, below a wooded area.

6. Fork right off the track just before a wedge of trees. Descend to pass more trees on your left. Reach a concrete lane.

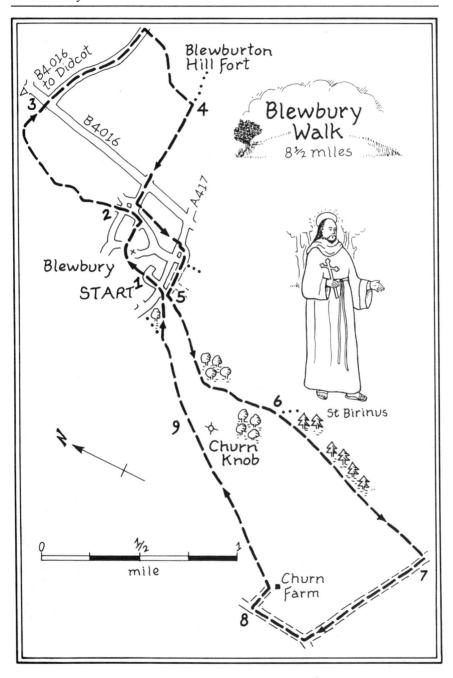

Blewburton
Hill Fort

Blewbury
Walk
8½ miles

B4016
to Didcot

B4016

A417

Blewbury
START

St Birinus

Churn
Knob

N

0   ½   1
mile

Churn
Farm

7. Turn right along the concrete lane and bear right with it at a junction with a lane on your left.

8. Turn right along the concrete lane signposted as a right of way to Blewbury. Pass a barn on your left and fork left along the path running beside a hedge on your right. Pass a track to Rose Cottage on your left, then reach a track below Churn Knob on your right.

9. With Churn Knob above and behind you on your right, take the hedged path ahead. Pass an old chalk pit on your left, bear right when you come to a fork and take a path with a hedge on your left and a fence on your right. Reach a junction and bear left to a road, cross it and take Nottingham Fee ahead, a road leading towards the church. Bear right along Chapel Lane to return to the Red Lion Inn.

St Michaels's Church, Blewbury

26. Wallingford

Route: Wallingford – Benson Lock – Shillingford Bridge – Slade End – Wallingford.

Distance: 6½ miles. Moderate.

Maps: OS Explorer 3 Chiltern Hills South or OS Pathfinder 1156 Henley-on-Thames and OS Pathfinder 1137 Watlington & Stokenchurch, plus OS Pathfinders 1136 Abingdon and 1155 Harwell, OS Landrangers 174 Newbury & Wantage and 175 Reading & Windsor.

Start: The George Hotel, Wallingford (SU 608895).

Access: Buses to Wallingford include no 105 (Reading – Oxford, tel. 01734 509509 or 01734 583747) and no 390 (Oxford – London, tel. 01865 727000).

The Tear Drop Room

Stay overnight in the Tear Drop Room at the George Hotel. It could lead to a rendez-vous with the inn-keeper's daughter. Unfortunately, she is a sad ghost of a girl who died over 300 years ago. Many have heard or seen her; more have felt a presence and been moved to pity. Royalist soldiers were billeted here during the Civil War. They were so rowdy that a gibbet was erected in the town square to give instant capital punishment to any soldier caught fighting in the town at night.

The inn-keeper at the George, a Mr Smith, was also under threat from the authorities for brewing his own beer. The local Justices of the Peace were dealing with Mr Smith when his beautiful daughter was to keep a date with a handsome Royalist sergeant, John Hobson. Distracted by the J.P.s, the inn-keeper and his daughter were not in the bar when some local ruffians picked a quarrel with Sergeant Hobson. Mindful of the gibbet, Hobson was unable to adequately defend himself in a fight. One of the ruffians stabbed and mortally wounded him. By the time Smith and his daughter arrived on the scene, Hobson lay dying in a pool of blood. His beautiful lover screamed and screamed. She then took to her room, out of her mind with grief.

For the rest of her short life, she stayed there and mixed soot from the fireplace with her tear drops. She drew beautiful tear drop shapes all over her bedroom wall and constantly whispered John Hobson's name. Eventually her strength left her and she died of lost love. Some of her tear drops remain, however, to be seen by guests staying in her old room. One man booked in for the night at the end of the 19th century without knowing the room's history. He awoke to an early morning thunderstorm. The flashes of lightning silhouetted a young girl tracing tear drop shapes on the wall. When she turned to face him, he saw a beautiful girl dressed in a white shroud and with black hair tumbling down her shoulders. Her face was pale and lonely, with wild, sad, eyes. Tears trickled mournfully down her cheeks. Going back to sleep, the man woke up much later, convinced he'd been dreaming. Then he saw a scattering of soot on the floor near the wall where the girl had stood. On the wall itself were fresh, 'black, tear drops. He called the landlord who, after hearing the traveller's tale, told him of the room's history. Her ghost was last seen in 1977.

The Icknield Way forded the Thames at Wallingford and there may have been a heroic struggle here between Britons and Saxons in the Dark Ages. It was the tyrant and usurper to the British throne, Vortigern, who invited Hengist and Horsa here and later became infatuated with Rowena. As a child, I remember learning that a sweet-shop in Wallingford used to be called Vertigern's. Could there be a connection? The Normans built a castle here to guard a bridge. The treaty ending the Civil War between Stephen and Matilda was signed here in 1154. It was one of the last Royalist centres to surrender to Cromwell, who then demolished it.

The Walk

1. Face the George Hotel and go right, towards the bridge over the Thames. Turn left just before the bridge to take the signposted Thames Path. This soon bears right off Castle Lane, going behind The Boathouse pub. It's worth diverting up Castle Lane first, to

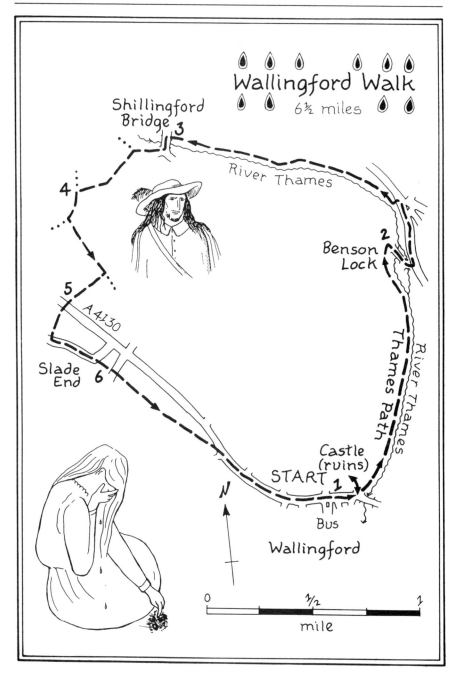

Wallingford Walk

6½ miles

Shillingford Bridge

River Thames

Benson Lock

A4130

Slade End

Thames Path

River Thames

Castle (ruins)

START

Bus

Wallingford

N

0   ½   1

mile

see the castle ruins on your left. Back on the Thames Path, walk
upstream with the river on your right.

2. Turn right to cross the river at Benson Lock. Go left with the
    Thames Path along a road and reach the A4074. Turn left, as
    signposted, through a gap in the hedge, reach the riverbank and
    turn right to walk upstream with the river on your left.

3. Turn left over Shillingford Bridge and turn right along a drive which
    passes Shillingford Bridge Hotel on your left and keeps above the
    river on your right. Go ahead along the track towards North Farm.
    Very soon bear left uphill and through a field. Bear slightly right in
    the next field.

4. Turn left along a grassy track which bears left to give fine views
    across the Thames Valley to the Chilterns. Walk with a high hedge
    on your right. Turn right at a track junction to pass a small orchard
    on your left.

5. Cross the A4130 and take a track waymarked as a footpath
    ahead. Keep ahead with a narrow path as the track bears right.
    Turn left along Sotwell Street, becoming Slade End. When this road
    bends left, go straight ahead along a path behind a cottage on
    your left and between garden fences.

6. Maintain your direction through a field, across a new by-pass and
    another field. Continue over a track and past backs of houses on
    your left. Emerge on Station Road (A4130) and go right along its
    pavement, immediately passing Fir Tree Avenue on your right.
    Continue along the High Street back to the George Hotel.

The path back to Wallingford from point 6

27. Henley-on-Thames

Route: Henley-on-Thames — Marsh Lock — Upper Bolney House — Harpsden — Henley-on-Thames.

Distance: 6½ miles. Easy.

Maps: Either OS Explorer 3 Chiltern Hills South or OS Pathfinder 1156 Henley-on-Thames, plus OS Pathfinder 1172 Reading, OS Landranger 175 Reading & Windsor.

Start: Blandy's House, Henley-on-Thames (SU 762826).

Access: Trains run to Henley from Twyford. Buses include no 390 (Oxford — London, tel. 01865 772250).

Mary Blandy

Mary Blandy was the only child of a widower, Francis Blandy, the Town Clerk of Henley-on-Thames and an Attorney-at-Law. She was 30 in 1749 and the thought must have occurred that she might be 'left on the shelf' in the marriage market. Perhaps because of this words were dropped that she could be worth a fortune. Mary came to the attention of a Scottish officer, Captain Cranston. Her father warned Mary that he'd heard that Cranston had a wife in Scotland, but she was obsessed with the Scotsman, who, in turn, had a devout interest in the Blandy fortune.

The sinister events started with the receipt of a package from Scotland, where Cranston had been recalled to duty, one morning in early August, 1651. It contained Scottish pebbles from which Mary was to make a pair of earrings, plus some powder for cleaning them. Mary was also keen on her father consuming this powder for some reason. She mixed it into his water-gruel. Unfortunately, he left the unfinished bowl on the table and a hungry washerwoman was made very ill by it. Mary then tried dissolving the powder in her father's tea, but it wouldn't, so she emptied it. Her slovenly chambermaid then used the unrinsed cup and was made ill by it. Not all of Mary's attempts to poison her father were failing, however, as his health visibly deteriorated and his bowels were very painful. By 9th August, even her father could guess what Mary was up to and confronted his daughter. She left the room in a hurry and he gave his tea to the cat, thus losing much sympathy.

He died on 14th August and Mary tried to destroy the evidence, burning Cranston's letters and dismissing the servants, while offering £500 to one to help her get away. The dead man's friends were soon informed, but little could be done as Mary was the new mistress of the house. She tried to leave town with £1000 in cash but was pursued by a crowd and sought refuge in the Angel pub that stood on the Berkshire side of the river. At this point the authorities detained her 'for her own protection', while the powder was identified as arsenic. Tried for murder, Mary Blandy was found guilty and hanged from the Castle Mound in Oxford (see Walk 14) on 6th April, 1752. She pleaded innocence as to the

The bridge at Henley

poisonous nature of the powder till the very end, believing her lover had sent it as an old Scottish love charm. Captain Cranston, meanwhile, had fled to Flanders, where he died of arsenic poisoning (suicide?) in December, 1752, the same year as Mary's execution.

The Walk

1. Face Blandy's House in Hart Street (now a dental surgeon's) and go right to pass St Mary's Church (where Mary Blandy is buried between her parents) on your left. Approach Henley Bridge, with a pub called the Angel on the Bridge on your right (but Mary most probably took refuge in another pub called the Angel on the far side of the bridge – that pub has now gone). Turn right to walk upstream with the river on your left.

2. Bear left with the signposted Thames Path, taking a footbridge to the Berkshire side at Marsh Lock and returning to Oxfordshire by a second footbridge. Continue walking downstream beside the Thames on your left.

3. Bear right away from the river and over a footbridge across a stream to follow an enclosed path, waymarked as the Thames Path. Bear right with a rough lane (Bolney Lane) and take a bridge over the railway.

4. Go ahead across a road and along a rough lane signposted as a bridleway. Go ahead across Woodlands Road to take a private road but public bridleway and follow this past Upper Bolney House on your left.

5. Turn sharply right, as waymarked by a painted white arrow. Go over a stile and walk beside a fence on your right. Cross a stile in the corner ahead and cut across the corner of a field to another stile. Go ahead along a fenced path to a stile beside a gate and take a

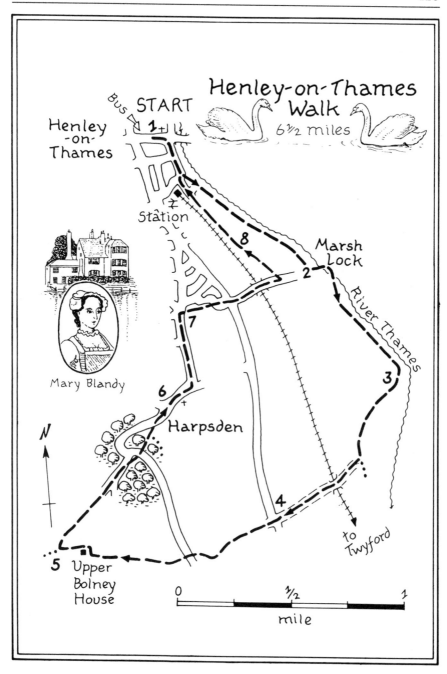

Henley-on-Thames
-on-
Thames

Bus

START

1

Henley-on-Thames
Walk
6½ miles

Station

Mary Blandy

N

Marsh
Lock

8

2

7

River Thames

3

6

Harpsden

4

to Twyford

5 Upper
Bolney
House

0   ½   1
mile

lane ahead. Follow it through woodland and bear right when directed by a white arrow painted on a tree, taking a woodland path. Follow more arrows on other trees to a road, go ahead across it and into more Woodland Trust land. Gradually converge with a road on your left and reach a road junction.

6. Bear right into Harpsden, passing St Margaret's Church on your right. Fork left along Harpsden Way and pass Rotherfield Road on your left.

7. Turn right along a signposted bridleway (Peppard Lane – an attractive path). Go ahead across the A4155 and go down Mill Lane. Cross the bridge over the railway and pass a football ground on your left, then turn left to walk through a car park. Take the signposted footpath from its far corner, going ahead beside a hedge on your right.

8. Go ahead with a shaded path between the railway on your left and the river meadow on your right. At the end of Meadow Road, turn right back to the riverside to retrace your steps past the Angel on the Bridge Inn and left to Blandy's House.

Also by Laurence Main:

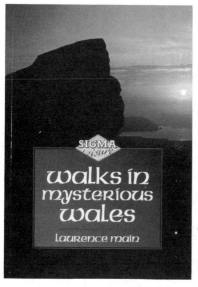

WALKS IN MYSTERIOUS WALES

The definitive guide to walking the very best parts of Wales and discovering the myths and legends of this ancient land. "An excellent book" – GLAMORGAN GAZETTE "Most Informative" – CAMBRIAN NEWS *£6.95*

WALKS IN MYSTERIOUS HAMPSHIRE

Enjoy downland views or plunge deep into dark forests of mighty oaks. Escape from modern civilization and emerge in the world of our pagan ancestors. *£6.95*

BEST PUB WALKS IN PEMBROKESHIRE

Ancient Pembrokeshire is a delight for walkers, with both seaside and inland walking. Plus the pleasures of local inns and Welsh Real Ale if you know where to look for it! *£6.95*

BEST PUB WALKS IN CORNWALL

Coastal and countryside walks, plus a Real Ale pub in every village that's visited. *£6.95*

BEST PUB WALKS IN THE COTSWOLDS

The longest-established and largest collection of real ale rambles for this attractive part of Britain. *£6.95*

BEST PUB WALKS IN SNOWDONIA

Mountain and valley walks from pubs that serve Real Ales. *£6.95*

More Sigma Books for The Heart Of England

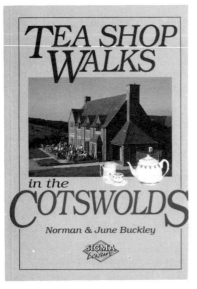

DISCOVERING COTSWOLD VILLAGES

This book by Gordon Ottewell is a practical guide to 50 of the most interesting and beautiful villages in the Cotswolds. Locals and tourists alike can discover the hidden delights of these superb English villages. With information about the architecture, history and wildlife plus snippets on local characters and folklore, you'll get the most out of a day on foot in the Cotswolds. *£6.95*

TEA SHOP WALKS IN THE COTSWOLDS

No other area in Britain has as many tea shops as the Cotswolds. This new book of 26 walks by Norman & June Buckley takes the reader the length and breadth of the area, visiting the popular towns and tiny villages. The walks average 5-6 miles and each features a tea shop that welcomes walkers. *£6.95*

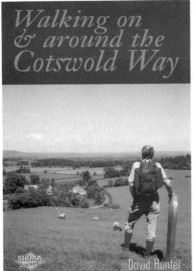

WALKING ON & AROUND THE COTSWOLD WAY

David Hunter's series of stimulating circular walks over 15 routes with excellent maps and photos. This is the leisurely way to walk "The Way"! *£6.95*

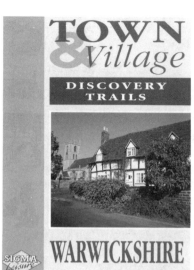

DISCOVERY WALKS IN WARWICKSHIRE

Explore this most historic of counties on foot with Dennis Kelsall. Find out about the county's wildlife, geology, climate, industrial heritage, architecture and history. Routes up to 10 miles intended as half or full day walks. *£6.95*

TOWN AND VILLAGE DISCOVERY TRAILS IN WARWICKSHIRE

Irene Boston's book is designed to appeal to residents and visitors alike: this varied collection of 40 trails visits some of the most attractive towns and villages in Warwickshire. Easy to follow and varying in length from half a mile to three miles. All the trails contain vital information on parking, public transport, tea-rooms, pubs and refreshments to make a visit as easy and fun as possible. With sections on nearby attractions and possible extensions to the walks, you can be sure that you aren't missing anything in this scenic and historical county. *£6.95*

EXPLORING STRATFORD-UPON-AVON: Historical Strolls around the town centre

John Abbott's enjoyable way to discover Shakespeare's Stratford - and much more besides. This fascinating and educational book takes you on walks along the river, into Stratford's streets and alleyways, in and out of its quaint inns and other ancient buildings, and to the many museums, gardens and architectural gems. There are also walks outside Stratford to attractions including Ann Hathaway's cottage at Shottery and Mary Arden's house at Wilmcote. *£6.95*